Diary of a rescue

Introductio

So, I am an 11 week old lurcher boy. My poor Mummy was made to have so many puppies in her life that the rescue centre managed to get hold of her and my Daddy and I was born in safety and was cared for properly. I went to stay with a foster family so that I could have a normal puppyhood while I waited for my forever sofa to come along, and indeed it did.

My new mum and dad lost their boy dog the day after I was born and they decided they would get another boy in a year or so, well, the very next day a picture of me magically appeared on Mums facebook and they ended up phoning the number and then came up to see me. They were told they had to bring their other two dogs up to meet me too in case they decided to give me a home. Rosie was really sad since Zak passed away and even had to go to the vet as she was so upset. So, as you can see, everyone liked me I think and the rest as they say is history.

My Mum and Dad keep saying, I can't remember what our other dogs were really like as puppies, so I thought I would write my own account of my first year as being a crazy little lurcher.

I hope you enjoy my tales of mischief and mayhem as I find my way in this thing called life.

Friday 20th July 2018

So there I was minding my own business and chasing bees in the garden and these 2 humans turned up with 2 other dogs. To be fair, I was a little bit scared at first but the humans got on the floor and said hello. I gradually approached the lady first and we had a bit of a play, she kept looking at me and smiling and I didn't worry so much after a while. Their dogs were just running abound and playing and didn't even consider saying hello.

I went inside with the humans and they all sat at the table with loads of bits of paper. They even drank water that had bubbles in it.

My foster mum gave the humans a bag with my food in it and also told them that they had to bring my teddy home with me. They had a little smile on their faces as they handed Teddy over.

Then suddenly I was picked up, and I went and sat on the lady's lap in this big weird box. The man started to make the box move and then the other 2 dogs just fell asleep on the sofa behind us.

For three and a half hours I sat in the box, which I now know is a car. I was pretty scared, but I just sat there quietly. The lady kept stroking me and giving me kisses.

Once the car stopped we went into a house, there I was greeted by a thing that I very soon learnt had knives on the end of its feet. It was not at all friendly but at least it was a bit smaller than me.

I was shown my new bed and pretty much that was it. I was so very tired so I curled up with Teddy and went to sleep after crying for the people to come back for half an hour. They didn't come back though so I ended up just drifting off to sleep in this new strange place.

Saturday 21st July.

So I was awake nice and early. I was taken out into my new garden. I found a little pond, it was so lovely I needed to take a closer look. Suddenly I was really wet, yep, I had fallen in. I went and dried myself off and then tried to make friends with the other dogs. I was sad as they kept running away from me. After a while one of them started to play with a toy so I took the opportunity to join in, well, that didn't quite pan out! She snapped at me and really scared me. I screamed at the top of my lungs and the lady (now known as Mum) picked me up and hugged me until I calmed down. I was so scared!!!!

I had a little nap and then when I awake, the thing with knives for feet started to follow me around. I thought she may want to be my friend so I went over to say hello. I couldn't believe it, she actually hit me on the nose. I was so shocked that I started to scream yet again. Mum came and got me and cuddled me until I stopped.

Later on in the evening, we all sat down in the room with the sofa in it and I watched a magic window. It was great, lots of interesting things to watch. Then I decided I would try and have a cuddle with the other dog. Oh my god, she growled at me. So I had another scream. I yet again got a cuddle until I felt better. Mum and Dad looked very tired so we all went to bed. I only cried for about half an hour and then curled up and slept with my teddy again.

Sunday 22nd July

Not a good morning. I had belly ache and I really need the loo, no one was around so I had to do it in my crate. Mum came down and saw me and let me out. We went in the garden and I went toilet again. When we got indoors again, Mum took out the mat in my bed and was muttering happy birthday to me whilst urging and scraping my pooh down the toilet. She then put it in the big white thing and covered it with water. She then took it outside.

Dad got up and had a play with me, he really loves me, I can tell.

There was a loud bang at the door, the other 2 dogs started to bark. I didn't know why. Then this lady walked in. She was cuddling the other dogs and ignoring me. I was not happy with this at all.

Well, I soon interrupted that and made it quite clear I needed to say hello. She was lovely, she gave me lots of cuddles and then I sat on her lap.

In the afternoon, the other 2 dogs started to do lots of stretches and lick their lips. I could smell lovely things so I went and sat and watched Dad making food. We all sat there watching them eat and then Mum went into the kitchen. Suddenly the other dogs started to jump around. They were getting a roast dinner with veg and gravy. Then Mum came out with my dish, it was full of chicken. It was very yummy.

After lunch I had a snooze on the sofa with the dog called Maizie. It was ok, she didn't yell at me and let me stay there.

Then later, Dad went and sat out in this thing called a hot tub. Mum sat on the step so I thought I would have a cuddle. She started to hold me really tight and water came out of her eyes. She said she had a boy again.

I went and investigated the garden again and was annoyed that my little pond had been fenced off. I really liked playing in that. Spoil all my fun they did.

Then I found some rocks in the garden, I was really shocked when I saw them start to move and didn't know what to do so I had a jolly good bark at them.

After a really nice day I went to bed and cuddled teddy and went to sleep.

Monday 23rd July

Yay, my belly is better!! I got up and Mum let me and the rest of the animals out, I had a couple of wees and a big pooh. Mum was running around acting a bit odd, she went in the big white thing and got all wet. It was very weird. Then Dad came down and gave me a cuddle. Mum suddenly picked up her computer thing and put it in a bag. Rosie looked very sad so I didn't know what was going on. Mum got up and went through the front door.

Then I was left with just Dad. He got out this weird machine, the other dogs ran to their beds. I really didn't know why. Suddenly the machine started to make a noise so I ran to my bed to take cover.

Hours later, Mum came home and then Dad went out. We went out into the garden and I played with fallen apples. I went to come back to the decking and the thing with knife paws which I have now learnt is called a cat, sat on the step looking at me as if to say "you can not pass this way". I was really scared so Mum came and got me. I managed also to climb onto the sofa in the garden, it was rocking, and very odd. But I really enjoyed playing on it and had good fun.

When I returned to the house, I got Teddy out of my crate, Mum and Dad thought it was very cute the way I played with him until they realised that Teddy was in fact my humping toy.

The main thing I learned today though was that what the cat eats is very tasty, the dogs all watch her and as soon as she finishes, they go and check if there is anything left. I got to have a taste too and it was yummy. I also realised that I am not the only one who is scared of the cat!

Well, another day over, so off to bed with Teddy again, and I only cried a little bit.

Tuesday 24th July

Epic day today, I found my running feet!!!!! I got up this morning and Mum was behaving the same as yesterday morning. I knew she was going to go out. I decided the best course of action was to keep wanting to go out in the garden. I thought I could make her forget to go out. It didn't work.

During the day I slept a bit, played a bit and then Dad put me in my crate and went out. I coped well.

Mum came home, I was so excited, I started to zoom around, she said I had turned into a little devil, I think that's a good thing. Granny came into see me, she seems scared of me. I wanted to play with her and she shouted because this red stuff came out of her hand.

Dad came home and went in that tub thing again so I decided to see just how fast I could go. I started at the bottom of the garden and ran like the wind, I then leapt off my feet and that's when it all went wrong. Suddenly I was in the big pond. I was a bit like Jesus as I managed to pretty much walk on water. As soon as I stopped I could feel myself sinking in the water so I started to scream. Mum pulled me out and carried me indoors. She then got a big towel and started to really rub me while I continued to scream. I then realised that actually it was quite nice to be rubbed and I calmed down. For the rest of the evening I slept on Mum's lap to get warm again.

What a day, I was so glad to go to bed, but what no one realised is that just before I did, I did a big pooh on the front door mat! Ha ha ha.

Wednesday 25th July

Today has been a really good day. Mum got up and discovered Dad had found my secret poop, he trod on it and then walked all through the house and up to the bedroom. She came down in the morning, let us all out for a wee and then started to clean my poop up. I love the cleaning game, I love trying to grab the cloth and also I like to try and get a piggy back too.

Mum then left for work so dad took us all out in the garden and also played with me. I got to do some sun bathing in the garden and I also like eating that pot of special dog grass that Mum has grown for us.

When Mum got home we went outside and I ran like the wind down the garden, Rosie followed me and we both did really fast whippety spins on the lawn. Rosie seems to like me now but I am still a bit scared as she is a lot bigger than me.

After I had my tea, Mum and Dad had some friends come over as they wanted to meet me!! They bought gifts and we all sat outside. I got lots of cuddles and got to play a lot. I really fancied Emma to be fair, she was very beautiful and I got all excited so decided to hump her arm! Everyone laughed but Dad came and stopped me.

We stayed up way past my bed time and I ended up falling asleep on Mum's lap.

After the people left I had supper and went to bed with Teddy and I slept like a log.

Thursday 27ᵗʰ July

So today I have realised there is a morning routine. I woke up at 6am and was swiftly assisted out for a wee. I was still very tired from the night before though so I decided to just go to sleep on the sofa. Rosie came and joined me.

After Mum had gone to work, Dad put all my toys away and got out that horrid hoover again. I ran into my crate and the others went to their beds too.

It was a pretty run of the mill afternoon and I dozed and played alternately.

Mum came home with a massive box today, it was all full of my puppy food, she also bought packs of grown up food the same as mine as she said she didn't want the others to feel like they were missing out and that they would love me faster if they could see the benefit of me being here. Cheek of it, of course there's a benefit. I am so damn cute to start with!

We went out into the garden and Rosie started to stamp her feet at me and chase me. I wanted to play but I hid as I got a bit scared. She is so much bigger than me.

Dad went out on his other Harley so I played loads with Mum. I think I made a bit of red stuff come out of her arm at one point. Then she decided to get me to play with my toys instead of her hand. My best toy at the moment is a ball with a bell in it. It belongs to the cat but I really love chasing it around the house. I did have a bit of a scream when I ran into the crate door as I didn't see it. Mum and dad laughed at me a lot.

I did some really good zoomies around the garden and I have learnt that sticking to running up the decking means I cant fall in the pond.

Well, all in all it was a pretty good evening and we all shared the front room until I went to bed with Teddy. I like it here I decided.

Friday 27ᵗʰ July

So yet again this morning we were up at the crack of dawn. I felt a bit sick this morning but Mum said it was because I was hungry so I got my wonderful dish of puppy food and gobbled it right down. Mum went out for the day again so I had the usual day of running away from that machine Dad pushes all over the floor. I played a lot with my toy that I stole off the cat and practiced my zoomies around the house. Later on Mum came home so I had a good play. Rosie is still attempting to get me to play but she does still scare me a bit as she is so big.

So I have been here a whole week now, I can't believe what I have learnt. I know that I am referred to as Harley, I know cats are grumpy little gits and that the other 2 dogs like me if I don't bother them too much.

I have learnt that my legs move really fast and that ponds get you very wet. I think I am really going to like my life here. But I really wonder what it is like on the other side of the front door. I have to wait 2 weeks before I can find out.

So I am very tired tonight, I have stayed up way past my bed time and watched dad bop around with big white things over his ears, I'm not sure what I think about that as he didn't seem to be able to hear me. Oh yeah, the other thing that I have sussed out this week, and to be fair, it is pretty amazing. There is a whole room in the house that is full of food, I have mastered climbing up to see what's about. I really need to get a bit taller though as then I will be able to reach all those nice things.

Saturday 28th July

This morning was odd, No one woke up. At 7.30 I thought I had better raise the alarm that everyone was late getting up. Mum came and let me out for a wee and then I curled up on the sofa with her and Rosie for a nap. Mum didn't go out!!!!

When dad got up I went and did more zoomies in the garden, but I misjudged a step and fell over. Everyone thought it was funny.

I also learnt how to play pulling games today, they are fun and Mum and Dad said I am getting stronger.

I found a plant today that I thought was tasty, apparently it's called a pineapple and seems to be special to Mum. I pulled it out of the pot and she gave me a smack on my bum. To be fair it wasn't hard but I decided to scream and limp so she picked me up and cuddled me. I have so nailed the guilt trip to be fair, get told off, scream and look maimed and suddenly I am completely forgiven!

Mum and Dad seem to think I may win an Oscar soon. They put a photo of me on facebook and so far I have 483 likes, whatever that means.

Today I learnt that my meat does taste ok with puppy mix so Mum and Dad don't have to do two courses anymore.

Well, off to be with Teddy I go. Night night.

Sunday 29th July

This morning started off very badly. I woke up hearing a really loud noise by my window, it really frightened me and I weed myself. I started to bark as Mum and Dad didn't seem to notice the noise. Mum came down and looked sad that I had weed the bed, but when she opened the door to let me out she sounded very shocked. The big gazebo that we sit under to stay out of the sun was upside down and half in Granny's garden. Dad and Granny were out in the rain taking it all apart while Mum cleaned my bed and gave me breakfast. They said I was a good boy for waking them up so I feel much better now.

I really don't like this wet stuff all over the garden, it appears to be falling out of the sky. I haven't seen that before, and now the big outside house thing is broken I didn't really want to go outside much.

Dad came in after the rain and I watching him cook that "roast" thing again, after they ate, they gave me puppy food and the others got roast. Highly unfair I think, they said it's because I have a delicate tummy, well, I'm a lurcher for god's sake. I can eat anything.

Later on the ground went dry again so I practiced my zoomies, I am getting better at it by the day, although I did run right into Mum at one point.

9

I am still really trying hard to be liked by the other two dogs and they seem to let me join in with more stuff every day, the cat however, she just looks down her nose at me. I have tried barking and she still ignores me. I will get there one day. Perhaps I may catch her a rabbit or something.

I have got used to the late nights so tonight I managed to stay up til 12.40am, I messed Dad around a bit as I really couldn't find myself a suitable wee spot in the dark.

Tonight I am going to have to be a brave boy when I go to bed as Teddy wont be with me. Because I weed on him they have punished him by putting him in some box with a round window at the front. I hope Teddy will be ok and that I get him back soon.

Monday 30th July

I woke up this morning when Mum came down, she took me out for a wee and then I lay on the sofa watching her get ready to go out for the day, before she left she gave me my breakfast. I now have my meat and biscuits together and it is really yummy.

I was a bit shocked when I saw the box that Teddy is in fill up with water. I was very scared for him. I was relieved when Dad let him back out. He now looks really clean and smells really nice. I am a happy boy to have him back.

I went out in the garden to play while Dad did some jobs and repaired the gazebo over the tub, the wind had broken it badly, it made my hairs stand on end remembering yesterday morning and how scared I was.

I played with Rosie for a while but she got grumpy and growled at me as I got a bit carried away with myself.

I went in and played with my toys until dad went out. Not long after dad went out Mum came home. I was so happy to see her. Its funny because when she comes home she says hello and Rosie also says hello. I think I may have to learn how to do that too.

We went out in the garden and I played with apples that were lying on the floor. I did lots of zoomies and Rosie joined in. I played for a while with her and then got a bit scared again as she is still big to me.

I went and hid under the swing and then discovered the cat was sat in one of the rattan chairs, I went to say Hi and she started to bat me with those knife feet. I think she was playing so we did that for quite a while and I didn't get hurt.

After tea, I played with my little ball for ages, it was fun and I ran up and down the whole house. I got really tired and decided to have a sleep. Dad then woke me up and took me into the garden for a wee.

I was overjoyed to find Teddy in my crate and snuggled up with him and went to sleep.

Tuesday 31st July

Today was a pretty good day. I woke up in the morning and cuddled up with Rosie on the sofa while Mum got ready for work. After she had gone, Dad gave me my breakfast and then took me out so I could go to the toilet.

The day went quite well. Well, I did make one weenie mistake. I managed to creep behind the cat and I caught her. All I wanted to do wanted hump her but she was not in the mood, luckily for me she was facing away from me so she managed to wriggle away and I didn't get hurt.

The day was spent playing and napping and I was quite happy with that.

When Mum came home she took me out into the garden and granny came in to say hello. I decided I would try and play with the cat again, but she was not impressed this time and hit me, so I ran off.

I then went and played chasing windfall apples at the bottom of the garden. It was brilliant because Rosie and Maizie joined in. I felt like a proper pack member. It was fab!!!

In the evening I played with the cat ball for ages and then had a really lovely nap in Mum's arms, it was lovely to be cuddled.

I then had my supper and went to bed as I was very tired. All in all a pretty good day apart from the cat hitting me.

Wednesday 1st August

This morning I got up and did a wee outside, Mum gave me my breakfast early and I got really crazy and played a lot. I wouldn't go out in the garden again so Dad took me out and sat with me for over an hour until I went to the toilet again.

Dad had to go out during the day so I was put into my crate. I wasn't overly impressed with this situation so I cried for quite a while. Luckily he wasn't gone for too long.

Mum came home with lots of food and then went out into the garden. Mum and Dad started to put the gazebo back up so I stayed out of the way as there was lots of bits of big metal being moved around.

I managed to find a way into the little pond again today and got tangled up in solar light wires. Dad came and blocked it off, a little while later I found another way in, Mum came to get me and put her glass on the step, as she got me out I managed to stick my nose in and taste what was in the glass, Mum told me off and made me jump and I knocked the glass over. She then ran and got the watering can and washed the drink away. I still wanted to taste it but it was only water. Mum said that only adults were allowed to drink out of glasses like that!

Later on we played the chasing apples game and then went indoors. Mum got on the floor with us and we all played. It was really funny because Rosie got really excited and behaved just like I do.

I had such a busy day and by the end of the evening I was very tired and enjoyed snuggling up to Teddy in bed.

Thursday 2nd August

Today I stayed in bed until Mum came and got me, I went out for a wee and then had a snuggle on the sofa for a bit. When I went out again Rosie and me did some zoomies. She is slowly getting used to me.

Later on Dad went out, he left a big thing under the table, and when he got back and looked at the thing his got upset. So what had happened was he came home and discovered I had eaten my bed. Then he saw why. Maizie had been running up to my crate and stamping and barking. Dad thought that I was bullied but said he would wait and see what Mum said.

When Mum came home she told him not to worry, Maizie just wanted to play and sort of felt safe doing so because I couldn't get out. They put a cover over my crate and said that next time they go out they will move all the toys so Maizie can't wind me up. They even said they may put her in the kitchen so she can't see me at all.

Well, after tea, we all went outside and I played with Rosie again, and also had a play with the cat. She still isn't very keen on me, but I will continue to work on that!

I got up on the sofa and had a cuddle with Mum but I got a bit excited and I humped her, she was very shocked and said no, but I did see her laughing!!!!

I went to bed and now have a nice new blanket instead of the foamy thing.

Friday 3rd August

This morning I got up when Mum came down, we went out into the garden and I went to the loo. I had breakfast and then Mum went out. She wasn't gone very long though and came home with lots of things.

Jamie came over on his motorbike and I saw dad putting lots of stuff onto his bike. Then I heard lots of noise and they went.

Mum went out in the garden and started to put the gazebo back up, she was very busy and it was very hot so we all stayed indoors and lay by the fan to keep cool. I really did have quite a lazy day.

Mum gave Teddy to granny in the afternoon, I was really upset that he had been taken away, about half an hour later granny came back with Teddy, it was brilliant. He had a new nose, I ate the plastic one off when I was in foster care, but now he has a lovely soft woolly nose. Mum said that because we had adopted Teddy too, that we needed to look after him and make him better.

At tea time a lady called Karen came over, Mum gave her a hug so I assume they are friends.

Mum gave us all our tea, I ate mine really quickly and then realised I needed a wee, Mum didn't notice and I didn't know what to do as I didn't want to get my nice new blanket wet. Then I had a really clever idea, I managed to wee in my supper dish! I thought that was a very clever idea.

We all went out into the garden and it was a lot cooler so we all had zoomies and played a lot.

I heard this awful sound and Rosie and Maizie ran down the garden barking, They told me it was cats fighting. It sounded even worse than when I scream.

Rosie wanted to play a lot but I got tired quite quickly so I hid under the hazel tree.

I did get a 2nd wind though and I got on the swing seat and chased my tail, I also got very angry with my back leg as it wouldn't leave me alone. Mum and Karen thought this was very funny.

Bedtime was a bit strange tonight. Karen went upstairs and Mum slept on the sofa with Rosie, she had a really nice soft blanket and a big bit of it was hanging on the floor so that's where I slept all night. We didn't go to bed til 2am so I think I will be very tired tomorrow.

Saturday 4th August

We woke up quite early this morning. I had a lovely sleep on Mum's blanket last night and Rosie slept on the sofa with Mum.

Karen got up and we were all really excited to see her again. We had our breakfast and then Rosie went into her crate and Mum picked me up and we went out of the front door. Mum unlocked the car and Karen got in. Mum then put me on Karen's lap and also got in the car. We started to move and I suddenly got really worried. Things were going through my head, why was I in the car without Rosie and Maizie? Were they taking me back to my foster parents? Had I done something wrong?

It was such a worry, but then as I was thinking this we stopped again, we had only been driving for 5 minutes. We got out of the car and Mum carried me into this big room, there was a big counter and two ladies were stood behind it. They started to make baby noises and I liked them straight away. They let me stand on the counter and lick their faces.

I then got taken into another room and a lady started asking mum lots of questions. She then started to stroke me, she looked in my ears, and then put this thing on my chest, it was like she was listening to it. It was very strange.

Then this other lady walked in, she was important, I could tell, she was like the top dog of the house. Her face lit up and she said "they didn't tell me it was you!" Mum started to smile and said "we said we would get another boy next year" and started to laugh. The lady then said "I am so very pleased to see this. Well, then it all got a bit funny, the lady who asked all the questions started to give me treats and then the other lady made my neck sting a bit. It was ok though and I didn't feel anything.

I had more cuddles with the ladies and then we got back in the car.

When we got home, Rosie and Maizie were so happy to see me. We ran up and down the garden together, then they started to play. They let me join in, I was so happy. It looks like they actually missed me.

After all the excitement I was really tired so I went to sleep on the decking for ages and didn't wake up til tea time.

After tea Karen and Mum got in the hot tub again so I went to sleep under the dining room table.

At bed time Karen went upstairs again and Mum and Rosie got a blanket and went to sleep on the sofa, Mum left a big bit of blanket lying on the floor so I decided to sleep on that all night. It was lovely.

Today was a really brilliant day. I feel that finally my hard work has paid off and I can see that the other two actually really like me. Mum said I was now a full pack member. How brilliant is that???

Sunday 5th August

We managed to stay asleep until 7.30 this morning. Karen got up and started to pack her bags while I had my breakfast.

Just as Karen was leaving I heard a really load roaring sound and Rosie and Mazie started to run around wagging their tails. It was Dad, he had come home!

Karen and Dad had a hug and then she went. I was sad to see her go and I hope I get to see her again soon as she is so much fun.

Dad made a real fuss of me, I heard Mum telling him that I had been a very good boy and that we have to stop fussing and start to trust him a bit more and stop worrying.

Later on, Dad started to cook roast again and after they ate theirs, we all got a roast. Mind you, I only got chicken as apparently I am too young for a proper roast. We then went out in the garden and I found another apple to play with. It was good fun. I was really tired though and when Rosie tried to play with me I didn.t want to.

Later in the evening, I was lying on Mum's lap and sucking her thumb, it was lovely. I woke up properly and got a bit playful. I didn't realise though that I was lying very close to the edge of the sofa, suddenly I was falling. Luckily for me Rosie was asleep next to Mum's feet and I landed on her.

She was very shocked and Mum said I had winded her. Rosie started to sneeze a lot but eventually calmed down and Mum said I had not hurt her.

Eventually we went to bed. I went back in my crate and really was not impressed. I had really enjoyed the last few nights of having mum downstairs. I thought if I cried a lot Mum would come and get me, but she didn't so I ended up just going to sleep.

Monday 6th August

This morning I woke up with a dodgy tummy. I think it was all the fun of the weekend catching up with me. All I really wanted was to stay in bed.

Dad gave me breakfast after Mum went to work but I really didn't fancy it today. I could see that dad was getting very worried and he even phoned Mum. Mum said for him not to worry.

I didn't eat my lunch either. I didn't really want Mum to go back to work and was just missing her.

Mum came home earlier than usual and I was so happy, we went out and played in the garden. She bought us balls with bells in and we all have a great time playing with them. Even Rosie played with a ball and Mum said she had never done that before.

I was so hungry at tea time so I ate all my tea really quickly and then went and sat right next to the cat and watched her eat her tea. I have worked out that if I sit quietly next to her she doesn't have a go at me and then I am first to get to lick her dish. Sometimes there is even a bit of her food left and that is great.

Mum took me out through the front door again today, she wanted me to meet more people. I met Tom and his partner who live in the flat, he was very happy to see me and gave me a lot of cuddles. Mum said he is a singer and may be famous one day so I think I will keep being nice to him. I also met a lady called Maureen, she was lovely and called me darling. I liked her very much. I heard Mum say that at the weekend I don't have to be held anymore and that I will actually be able to go out to explore with the other dogs. I am really quite excited about that, but also a little bit scared. I wonder what happens when we go out, and also where we go. Oh well, I suppose I don't have long to wait to see.

In the evening I worked out that I am definitely not the same as the other dogs. I have these weird things growing between my legs, they are very off putting and I ended up playing with them for a long time. Mum and Dad were laughing a lot. They said something about not worrying as they won't be there for long. I don't quite understand that comment but I'm sure it's nothing to worry about.

I went to bed after Mum last night, Dad stayed up just to make sure I didn't need another wee before bed.

Tuesday 7th August

This morning I woke up and went out for a wee, then I decided to have a quick nap on the sofa. Mum gave me my breakfast before she went to work and then I decided to show dad that I would not mope around the house today. I got up to all sorts. I played with the cat, who to be fair, still isn't keen on me. I also went exploring the parts of the house I hadn't really bothered with before.

Dad said it was very tiring looking after me today because I was being so busy. Mum came home from work earlier and she had lots of balls with her. There were loads of them and she threw them all onto the floor. We all had a good play with them and then went outside.

Mum was cleaning out the fish pump thing, she said it really needed doing because I had taken up all her time over the last few weeks. Cheek of it, she could have still done that. The water that Mum was putting in the bucket smelt very interesting. Mum kept telling me to go away but I was really wanting to help. She went inside to clean some bits in the sink and I found a big sponge to play with. When Mum came back out she saw me playing with the sponge and came and took it away. I was really annoyed so I went indoors.

Rosie was happy to see me come in and started to play, we ran all over the house and did zoomies around the dining room table. It was great fun and we made loads of noise.

I managed to keep playing right up until bedtime, I chewed Dad's feet, played with the other dogs and then played with Teddy until we all went to bed.

Wednesday 8th August

I woke up this morning when Mum came and let me out. I did my usual get up on the sofa routine and slept until breakfast time.

After breakfast Dad went out into the garden and put feet onto the gazebo. It was great fun and I tried to help him as much as possible. I helped by carrying bolts around and climbing on to Dad's back to help steady him. He then started to use something called a drill. I really didn't like that. It was very noisy and frightened me a bit. I was glad when Dad had finished that.

I had a lovely power nap in the afternoon until Mum came home. We then went out into the garden and we all played together. It was great fun running as part of a pack. Rosie wanted to play loads.

Maizie ran in doors with a toy and I followed her in, I tried to take the toy and she told me off. I screamed and screamed, her telling me off made me jump so much. Rosie and Mum came running in and Mum picked me up and cuddled me. Rosie was really concerned and started to bark until she could see I was ok. Poor Maizie lay in her bed with a "I didn't touch him" look about her.

We went back outside and had another play and I soon forgot about the incident with Maizie.

After tea, we snuggled on the sofa for ages and then I had my usual evening play. Mum and Rosie were on the sofa. I went up to say hello and Rosie put her paw on my head. It was very strange because when she did that, mum burst into tears. She said it was because she never thought

Rosie would do that again after Zak went to rainbow bridge. Mum said Rosie has totally accepted me for her to actually do that.

At the end of the night I went to bed and snuggled down with Teddy.

Thursday 9th August

I am now getting this morning routine well sussed. I got up, had a wee and then curled up on the sofa with Rosie.

After breakfast I had a good play out in the garden with the other dogs. It was pretty windy and the cat got really weird. She started running around the decking and started to dive bomb me. I was pretty scared because I know that she has those sharp knives on her feet. She chased me around the garden for ages.

After my afternoon nap Mum came home. We went outside again and Rosie and Maizie played with me a lot and we ran up and down, It was brilliant, we ran and barked and played for ages. I got really tired and after tea I went to sleep.

I was then awoken by the dogs barking as someone was at the door. It was one of Mum and Dad's friends and she had a little person with her. I have never seen a little person before, he looked just like a normal person but was only half the size and his voice was really high too.

The little person got all excited to see me and started making screaming noises, to me that was an invitation to play. I jumped all over him and tried to eat his shoes. Mum and Dad then spent time talking to their friend who is called Parlsa and I discovered the little person was called Emil.

I was a bit annoyed as Parsla had a tub with sausages in, she gave them to Rosie and Maizie and Dad said I wasn't allowed any. I really need to hurry up and get big so that I can eat all the lovely things that the others eat. They eat some of my puppy food, yet I can't have any of their food. Unfair!

After Parsla and Emil went, Mum and Dad had tea and then watched the big window on the wall again. I still can't believe all the things that you can see out of that window, it's like magic.

I was really tired this evening so I went to bed with Teddy fairly early.

Friday 10th August

Today I got up when Mum came down. It was raining hard.t and I don't like the feeling I get when it all lands on me.

I had a pretty much run of the mill day, I played a while, slept a while and ate my meals.

Mum came home and it had stopped raining a bit so I went and played in the garden. Everything was still a bit wet though and I really am not keen. Our swing sweat was also wet so I couldn't even play on that. After tea, Dad went out and me and Rosie played loads, it was good fun and I am getting braver, she does tend to growl a lot when she is playing and I think she is telling me I need to do the same. Mum is really proud of me because I have now learnt to sit down when she asks me to. It's good fun as I get a treat when I do it.

I also got to go out of the front door. Mum carried me outside and then I just couldn't believe it! She put me on the floor, I started to talk about and realised I had a rope like thing attached to my collar, and Mum was holding the other end. We walked up and down the road a bit and Mum said I was a very good boy as I didn't really fight the rope. I saw another neighbour but was annoyed as he was in a rush and didn't really want to say hello. I also met the lady who lives on the other side of the fence, she gave me loads of cuddles.

When we came back in the house, we went in the garden and mum opened the gate to the other garden where Yoyo the big dog lives. Mum let me go in, I chased Yoyo through the garden and in though her house, when we got in the house I found Granny sat in her chair, she was very happy to see me and was laughing that Yoyo was running away from me. I had a jolly good sniff around Granny's house and then went back to our house.

When Dad came home he was acting a bit funny, Mum said it was because he had been to the pub. Mum really wanted to go to bed early and said she was very tired so Dad said he would stay up until I had been to the toilet so she could get a lay in. Well, I don't want Mum to have a lay in. I like getting up early. I eventually decided to have a wee at 3am as I couldn't hold it in any longer. It was horrible, I don't like the dark much and I really hate the rain.

I dried off a bit and went to bed with Teddy

Saturday 11th August

Today Mum didn't get up at her usual time. I waited for ages and then at around 7am I thought I had best at everyone was still in bed. Mum got up and opened the back door to let me go out for a wee. Well, I really wasn't happy as all that wet stuff was still falling out of the sky. I had a quick wee and then after breakfast I played for about 2 hours with Rosie, Mum kept saying "shhhhh" because we were getting very loud.

We both got so tired that we went to sleep after on the sofa, Mum was getting concerned as I was refusing to do a pooh. I didn't want to stay outside and get wet so I just decided I would go as long as possible without going.

I stayed dozing on the sofa for most of the day and then finally went and did a pooh just before tea time. I am still confused with the dog flap, the others just go in and out but when I try the door stays shut. Mum said I have to push it with my nose, but I just can't work out how. She held it open for me and I went out through it and then she did the same so I could get back in. Perhaps I will try again tomorrow.

I had such a lazy day today. I was supposed to go for my first walk today, no chance. I don't want to get wet, and the other two dogs didn't want to go either.

Mum filled up the big white thing with water today and then she got in it. We all came and rested our heads on the edge of the bath and watched Mum. Then she got this little thing and it squired water at Maizie and Rosie, they tried to catch the water, it was really funny, Mum let me have a go, I wasn't very good. She then took photos of us and laughed and said that the bathroom perverts were back. Aparently, it is something she used to do with Zak, he is Mums old dog who died the day after I was born. Mum said baths were horrid after he went because she felt lonely. I am so glad I could make Mum feel happy again.

After the bath I got to try pizza crust and also had a cheese and onion crisp. That was pretty cool. I have learned that human food is a lot different to my food and there are so many different flavours. I'm quite looking forward to trying more food.

I had to go out again in the rain before bed and I took ages to have a wee, I still get scared in the dark and then I got told off as I did a wee in the house. I don't normally but I think that it was unfair to send me out in the dark and rain and make me wee.

I eventually went to bed with Teddy and curled up with him and went to sleep.

Sunday 12th August

So I woke Mum up again this morning just after 7am, she got up and went to let me out. Well, I have never seen anything like it. There was water everywhere, even Rosie stood looking outside in disbelief at how much water was falling out of the sky. I couldn't cope with going out there so I sneaked off into the hallway and did my wee there. I was bursting. Rosie kept looking outside and then at one point decided she couldn't wait any longer. She came back in a few minutes later and she was soaked to the skin.

Mum decided that I had to get used to the rain so every hour she took me out in it. I really didn't like it, and also the gazebo roof had collapsed with all the water. Mum got a knife and put a hole in the material, I have never seen so much water, I had to run away.

After lunch the rain stopped, I had my first proper game of tug of war with Rosie and then we went out in the garden. The gazebo cover had been taken down and put under the swing. It was brilliant, I played in it and then Rosie joined me. We played for about 2 hours and had an amazing time.

Then Mum got all the leads out, this time there was a smaller one. Guess what? It was for me. Rosie and Mazie got all excited and ran to the front door. Mum put our leads on and then I went outside with them. I bounced around a bit but then the dogs stood either side of me and we all walked up the hill together. It was fab. We walked up and down three streets, mum said I can't go far yet as my legs are still not strong enough.

I saw lots of houses and cars, they go past very fast so I was a bit nervous to start but then I saw that Rosie and Maizie didn't really take any notice.

When we got home I played some more, well, pretty much up until bed time. Mum said she was proud as I had mastered going out in the rain. I get a treat every time I go out to the toilet, how fab is that!

I was pretty much pooped out by 10pm so mum took me for a wee and then I curled up in bed with Teddy again. It was a brilliant day and I am so happy that Rosie really loves me.

Monday 13th August

This morning I got woken up by Mum at 5.45 so I guessed it was a work day, se let me out into the garden and I had my morning wee. Mum went to work and then Dad gave me my breakfast as per usual. I had a good play in the garden with Rosie and then had a morning nap while Dad did all the house work. After lunch, Dad put me in the car again. Where was I going this time? It was only me again, the other dogs were left at home. I wasn't quite sure what was going on. Dad parked in a big carpark, it looked a bit like the one at the vets. He got me out of the car and carried me into a big building. He opened the door and there were four ladies in there, it took me a while to suss it out but then I suddenly realised that one of the ladies was Mum!

I had a good look around the office and said hello to Marie and Sarah, they said I was very cute. I thought they were very cute too. They both had lovely long hair and I really wanted to play with it. They were very kind to me and I liked them very much. I got some treats and one of the ladies had bought me a new toy. I then went and fell asleep behind Mum's chair until it was time to go home.

Mum drove us home, I didn't know where I was going again. Mum had to help me out of the car as I was a bit nervous, and then she opened the door and I realised we were home. I ran straight to Rosie's crate and was very happy to see her.

We all went out into the garden and I had a good play with Rosie again, Mum joined in and so did Maizie and we did zoomies around the garden.

After tea, I thought that because all the others had a play that I could get the cat to join in. I don't understand why she still won't play with me. She started to make a hissy sound at me and mum got really annoyed. She kept telling me off. I think I really upset mum as she got quiet and just sat on the sofa stroking Rosie.

Mum took me out for a wee and then I went to bed. I was pretty tired so I didn't cry when I went to bed, I just cuddled up with Teddy and went straight to sleep.

Tuesday 14th August

I got up at the usual time this morning and went right out for a wee. When I got back in I snuggled up on the sofa with Rosie. I now have this morning routine sussed and know Mum has to get ready for work. Dad got up and I was at the door to greet him. He made me my breakfast and then me and Rosie went out to play.

We pretty much played all day. Mum came home and did some stuff in the garden, I found a new place to explore around the other side of the pond. Mum looked a bit worried but I can assure her I won't fall in there again.

Mum then took me to the mystery door, it's the door they go to at night and I don't see them again until morning. She went through the door and left it wide open. I decided to be brave and have a look. It was really weird, Mum was at the top of a very steep hill. I couldn't work out how she got up there. She started to call me but I didn't know what to do. Suddenly Rosie ran past me and went straight up the hill, so I followed her. I took it very slowly and boy was that a climb! So I got to the top of the hill and had a look around. I found Mum and Dad's bed, it is massive compared to mine. I wonder if I will ever get a bed that big.

Rosie and Mum went back down stairs and I stood at the top not knowing how to get down. Then Mum started telling me it was all ok so I went down one step at a time, it felt very strange with my head so far down and my bum in the air behind me, but I did it. Mum was very pleased. We did that again a few times and it just got easier.

After tea I had more play time and then eventually got really tired so I had supper and went to bed with Teddy.

Wednesday 15th August

Usual routine this morning. Mum woke me up and I had my morning wee. I then snuggled up on the sofa for a doze until breakfast time. After Mum went to work, Dad gave me breakfast and then I had a play with Rosie.

Just before lunch, Dad got out the ropes again and we all went for a walk. It was great seeing all the new things, well, apart from a little person who started shouting that she hated dogs to her mum. Well to be fair, we didn't like you much either you little brat. We were walking along and could hear this loud noise, Dad decided it might scare me so we went a different way. Rosie and Maizie walk either side of me. I love being in the middle, it makes me feel safe.

When we got home we had lunch and then I slept for a bit. When I woke up me and Rosie had another play until Mum came home.

After Mum came home, Dad went out on his bike for a ride so we all went into the garden as Mum said we were being to boisterous in the house. I didn't understand what she meant by that. We went out and me and Rosie played under the swing. Rosie got so excited she started spinning around really fast and then managed to jump 8ft right over the pond and ran down the garden. I followed her as quickly as I could and then we both ran and span around together. It was great fun. I think Maizie got a bit worried and came down to calm us down.

After tea we all slept for a while, then we had another play, Maizie actually played with me for a brief moment too. It was great.

I dozes a lot in the evening as I was very tired with all I did today. Dad gave us our supper and I managed to steal some of the other 2 dog's food. I then went to bed with Teddy and everything was fine until about midnight when I woke up with belly ache. I started to bark because I really needed the toilet, Mum came down and took me into the garden. I just about made it. Then I went back to bed and fell asleep.

Thursday 16th August

Well what a night I've had, I awoke at around midnight with a very bad tummy ache and I really needed the loo. I was in my crate so I had to raise the alarm. I started to cry and Mum came down and let me out. I rushed out into the garden and had a massive pooh. I was so relieved she let me out. Well, it didn't stop there, every time I got settled back in bed my tummy started to make noises and I had to keep alerting Mum and Dad to come and get me. It was a horrible night, it was wet outside but I had to just put up with it. At 5am Mum let me out again and then stayed up with me. My tummy started to feel a little more settled. Mum and Dad tried to explain to me that stealing Rosie's tea had done this to me as I am too little to eat grown up dog food. But I really like it so I wish I could get big quickly.

After Mum went to work Dad told Granny what happened last night, she gave me this nice tasting stuff, it was to make me better apparently. It was yummy. I had breakfast and then dosed on the sofa for a while.

I woke up and had a play with Rosie, I felt a bit rough still but I didn't have belly ache anymore. Mum came home really early today so we went out in the garden and had a play. We didn't go for a walk today in case I needed to pooh again as mum said she wouldn't be able to pick it up. Why would she want to pick my pooh up, that's just weird.

Well, me and Rosie came in and started playing a lot, then I ran like crazy and landed on Mum, I fell backwards and Mum made a really loud noise and started to hold her face. I felt really bad, I had hurt mum. It turns out my head hit her on the nose really hard and I could see her eyes were swelling up. I gave her lots of kisses to try and say sorry.

Mum then took us back out side and Maizie was acting a bit funny, I couldn't tell is she wanted to play with us or if she was angry. Mum took me and Rosie inside and then went out and played ball with Maizie for ages. Mum said she needs one to one play sometimes. After they finished, Mum put this thing over Maizie's nose, it's called a muzzle. Maizie could then join in with us so she couldn't get to excited and bite us.

We had our tea after that and then all chilled out in front of that magic window thing. When it got late, Muma and Dad woke me up and made me play, they said they needed to get a good sleep. Well so did I, I was pretty tired after being up all night too. They gave me more of that medicine and then I curled up in bed with Teddy and went straight to sleep.

Friday 17th August

Today I was woken up by Mum at the usual time. I went and had a wee and then slept on the sofa with Rosie. I had breakfast and then went and played outside with Rosie when the hoover came out. Got I hate that thing. I can't believe Dad doesn't try and attack it. I think when I get bigger I will try my best to kill it so it leaves Dad alone.

I had my usual day and then Dad put me in my crate and went out. I was only in it for about half an hour and then Mum came home. I was so excited to see her, and I jumped and jumped but she said no and then crouched down so I could say hello properly.

There was a knock at the door and I got confused. Mum didn't answer the door, she climbed onto the window sill and opened the window and a man gave her a parcel. Mum opened the parcel and there was a bottle in it. Apparently, it is calming drops for Maizie. Maizie seemed to really like it but I wasn't allowed a taste.

We all went and played in the garden until tea time and Maizie even tried to join in a little bit, but I think she is still a bit scared of me. I think she realises that one day I will be bigger than her.

After tea we went out and played again. Maizie stayed in as she didn't want to play. I discovered a nice patch of earth at the back of the pond, so I sneaked across and started to dig a hole. Mum told me off, so I carefully walked back over to the garden. A bit later Rossie decided to have a look at what I had been doing. Mum told her off for going there and she nearly jumped over the pond. Instead she walked back along the edge, and I couldn't believe it. She lost her footing and fell in the pond. Her back legs were in there and she stayed still and just waited for mum to pull her out. Mum said she couldn't believe Rosie did that as she had lived here for six years and had never fallen in. She said it was my fault for leading her astray. Huh, Rosie doesn't have to do what I do so I am not taking the blame for that.

In the late evening we chilled out on the sofa, had a doze and then after supper I went to bed and cuddled up with Teddy again.

Saturday 19th August

This morning Mum didn't get up at her usual time. So I waited until 7.15 and thought I had better raise the alarm that everyone had overslept.

Mum came down and let me out for a wee and then I got on the sofa for my usual nap. Mum didn't get ready for work. I think I am working out that she goes to work most of the time and then has a couple of days where she stays at home. It seems to be called "the weekend".

I had breakfast and then I went outside for a play. Mum pulled up a lot of plants in the garden and was putting them in a big sack, I tried to help by trying to take them back out of the sack. She then tried several times to block off the side of the pond, but I kept showing her it wasn't working.

Maizie came out and joined us and she actually played pull games with me. That was good and Mum was pleased but it didn't last long.

Dad went away to stay with some friends so we carried on playing in the garden. Mum put Maizie's muzzle on her and I must say, I am glad she did. Me and Rosie were playing and Maizie came and barged into me. Rosie was not happy about this and chased Mazie away, but they had a fight. Mum stepped in and stopped them and took us all inside. Rosie wants to protect me all the time but I got a bit sad as I think Maizie was just over excited with play. Mum and Dad keep saying her brain isn't the same as a normal dog.

We all came in and chilled out and watched some spooky films. Then mum got the white bag out and Rosie and Maize and the cat all had prawn crackers. I was only allowed a little bit because of my little belly only liking puppy food. Several times the other dogs kept running to the door thinking Dad was back. Mum kept telling them he would be back tomorrow but they wouldn't listen.

Mum told Rosie it was very nice that she looks after me but when Dad is away, Mum is the boss, not Rosie. She got it in the end.

We had supper and then we all went to bed and I cuddled up with Teddy.

Sunday 19th August

This morning I raised the alarm at 7.15 as Mum was still in bed. I was a bit confused as Dad never came home last night. All very odd. I had some breakfast and then went and had a play in the garden. I still keep trying to get back to the hole I started to dig, but Mum still keeps telling me off.

Mum gave us all a chew so she could watch the magic window on the wall and I was really enjoying mine until Maizie decided she wanted it. She took it from me and barked, I got really scared and ran through the house screaming. Rosie looked all confused and started to bark. Mum gave me a cuddle and I felt better and stopped screaming. I got my chew back and carried on eating it.

Not long after the front door opened. It was Dad, he was back. I was so excited by this. He said hello to us all and then started to cook the big dinner that he always seems to do on a Sunday.

After lunch we played and played, Rosie seemed a bit tired today but she still tried to play a lot to keep me amused.

Today was a pretty boring really, but in a way that's a good thing because it means I didn't get into any trouble.

After tea, we had another play and then I went to bed with Teddy.

Monday 20th August

Today I got up again at the usual time. I had my morning wee and then settled down on the sofa with Rosie while Mum got ready for work. After breakfast I want ed to play but Rosie just didn't want to. I don't know why she didn't want to play and so I just messed around by myself and amused myself.

Dad did the hoover thing and then played with me in the garden. He kept telling me I was naughty when I tried to eat more plants so I decided to have a snooze.

In the late afternoon Dad put me in my crate, I wasn't in there for long before mum came home and let me back out of the crate. Rosie came and greeted me and we started to play. We played a lot and when Dad came home he told Mum that Rosie had been very quiet today. Mum said she seemed fine again.

After tea, I decided to try yet again to make friends with the cat. I kept going up and saying hello to her but she just kept hitting me. Every time I went away from her she would follow me so I would try again to say hello but she would then hit me again. Although I have noticed that when she hits me her knives don't come out so she can't hate me that much.

I was quite tired this evening so I spent most of the evening sleeping in the front room with the other dogs. I think that when I am asleep I grow quicker. I know I am getting bigger as I am nearly the same size as Rosie now.

At around 10.30 Dad took me out into the garden for my last wee and then I went to bed with Teddy, It was very comfy as I had rearranged my bed myself a while earlier.

Tuesday 21st August

This morning Mum came down as usual and let us all out for a wee. We then did the usual routine of dozing on the sofa.

After breakfast, Dad got the rope things out again and we all went out. We walked all the way along a very long street of houses, they all had drives and I wanted to explore each and every one of them. Rosie and Maizie made me walk in the middle to stop this. We walked for ages and to be fair, I got pretty tired out. But it is great getting to see everything on the other side of the front door.

When we got back I slept out in the sun with Rosie for ages, it was lovely feeling the warmth of the sun on my coat.

Dad put me in the crate later but again, I wasn't in there for long and then Mum came home. We were all really excited and all started to play again. Me and Rosie played but with less effort as we were both still tired. We ended up just cuddling on the floor. Mum says Rosie really loves me, well that's brilliant because I love her too.

When Dad came home, Mum told him that one of my brothers or sisters had something called a DNA test and that we had found out what mix of dog I am. They were both laughing and saying that I may become a very big boy.

After tea, Rosie didn't want to play anymore, so I decided to see if the cat wanted to play instead. I know mum gets worried as the cat is very old, but she seemed ok and played with me for quite a while. And no knives came out of her hands so I think she was happy to play.

I had a pretty early night tonight due to being on the go all day, it's been a great day today and I had lots of fun. I went to bed after my night time wee and cuddled up with Teddy.

Wednesday 22nd August

I got up at the usual time this morning and was let out for a wee by Mum. I then did my usual dozing on the sofa with Rosie.

After mum went to work I had breakfast and then had a little play with Rosie. Dad decided today to teach me how to use the dogflap. He held the door open for me and I eventually sussed it out.

I think Dad came to regret it as he heard a splash and realised I had fallen in the pond again. Dad had fenced it all off but I thought I would still manage to jump over it.

Mum came home with a massive bunch of flowers, they were for a lady called Lisa who had painted a picture of Zak for Mum and Dad. The house smelt lovely. Its just a shame we won't be keeping them.

Mum weighed me today and I am 11.4kg already and Dad told her he had been researching longdogs today. I think he means me.

In the evening I played with Rosie a lot again and then I went out through the dog flap to have my bedtime wee before snuggling down with Teddy in my crate.

Thursday 23rd August

When I got up this morning I thought I would break up my morning routine. So instead of dozing on the sofa, I went outside with Rosie and played for a good hour. It was fun and we chased each other all over the garden.

Dad was impressed that I still remembered how to use the dog flap, but he kept coming outside with me as he doesn't trust me not to fall in the pond or eat plants that I shouldn't.

Mum came home early today, she had been up to see a friend and took those lovely flowers with her. She said it felt quiet when she got home as she had been at a house with 10 dogs.

We played a lot again, Maizie really looks like she wants to join in but Mum still puts her muzzle on in case she gets too excited as she doesn't want me to get hurt.   I did get hurt today though. I played with the cat again today, but she ended up getting really cross and hit me. This time the knives were out and she hurt me. I screamed for a bit but I was ok. I think I was just shocked that the cat could do that to me.

In the evening I slipped out through the dog flap, Mum wondered where I was so she came looking for me. Oh oh, I was in trouble. I had found a lose bit of earth under the gravel at the bottom of the garden so I dug a big hole. Mum was annoyed with me and picked me up and carried me back in doors. I had already got a plant of the outdoor table earlier and spread earth every where so I was in the bad books.

We came in doors and I cuddled up with Mum, it was great, she just can't stay mad at me. She took more photos of me as well because my ears are so strange still.

Anyway, after my wee I went to bed and cuddled up with Teddy.

Friday 24th August

I got up this morning when Mum came down. This morning I thought I should go back to my usual routine of chilling out on the sofa until Dad got up and Mum went to work.

Dad gave me my breakfast and then I decided today would be the day that I got to do what I wanted.

I went out into the garden and saw that the hole I had dug had been filled in and that a big bit of wood was lying over the spot where it was. Ok, so what should I do instead. I know, I thought I would see what was under the lawn. It's a weird lawn, not like the one at my foster parents. This lawn seems a bit strange, well it's like a carpet. I pulled at it and realised I could move it. When Dad came out he told me off and said "No" really loudly. I was not happy with this. I wanted to see what was under the lawn.

When Mum got home, Dad told her that I had been naughty all day and he had to keep a proper eye on me. Naughty? Really?? I was just investigating things and I really did want to know what was under the lawn. There could be some prime digging land under it. Maybe I will try again once I look like I have lost interest and then I can find out for sure.

In the evening I played with Rosie a lot and then had my tea. I tried yet again to get the cat to play with me, but she just kept hitting me and then she hissed at me too.

Once I settled down on the sofa with Rosie, the cat (who I have learnt is called Bunky) decided she would come and sit next to me. I was really scared but I am not going to let her know that.

I went out for a wee last thing and then came back in to my crate and settled down to sleep with Teddy.

Oh, one last thing. I have officially mastered the dog flap. It's brilliant as I can now come and go as I please. Massive achievement.

Saturday 25th August

I woke up this morning on my own and got very concerned that Mum wasn't up yet. So I started to bark a bit so that she got up. She came down stairs, it was around 6am. "Harley" she said, "I don't have to be up early today". Ooops, well at least if she had got it wrong then I had got her up in time. Dad got up not long after, and went out hunting, or as you humans call it "shopping". He came back with lots of nice stuff and I had my breakfast.

Mum got ready to go out and then got my lead out. She took me out to the car. I really don't like getting in and out of that, and I was concerned as the other dogs and Dad stayed at home. All sorts of things went through my mind, was I going back to my foster parents? Was I going to the vet? Well it didn't take long to find out where I was going. Mum parked up and helped me out of the car. We were going into a massive building. When I got in there, I couldn't believe my eyes or nose. Gosh that place smelt fab, there were dog toys and chews everywhere. I was in heaven surely!

We went over to the bit where there there were leads and collars, Mum picked out a whippet collar, it was too small. She ended up having to get me a greyhound one, then I heard her tell someone I was half greyhound. They sounded impressed. Lots of people came and spoke too me and smoothed me. They all smiled and were very happy to see me. I felt really important.

We left the shop and drove back home. Mum had bought the other dogs some treats and gave them some. It was a lovely sunny day so we all went out in the garden. Mum put the blanket from the swing on the decking and we all sunbathed and played on it. It was lovely.

Mum also took lots of photos today and her friends were all shocked too see how big I have got. I am now nearly the same size as the other two dogs.

We played until it got a bit cold and dark and then Mum bought the blanket inside and we all continued to play until bed time.

Today was a really good day and I want to go back to that shop again and see what I can find to bring home. I stayed up quite late tonight but eventually went out for a wee before settling down for the night with Teddy.

Sunday 26th August

This morning I woke up at 6.45am and gave Mum a shout so she would get up. It was really raining and horrible outside so I did a quick wee and then came back in doors. I played a lot with Rosie and Mum had bought the blanket inside and put it on the floor so we could play on that. It was a pretty quiet day due to the rubbish weather.

In the evening Mum and Dad's friends came over. I had met Jamie and Parsla before but there were also two boys with them. Parsla came with a big tub of sausages, and started to give them to Rosie and Maizie, Mum said I was allowed to have one. It was yummy. The two boys, Dylan and Steven said hello to me and then started to play with me, it was great fun.

Later on there was a knock at the door and a load of food arrived. There were prawn crackers, I love them. I was allowed a little bit. After they had finished eating, Parsla gave me a toy she had made with crochet, Rosie and Maizie were sad that they didn't get one. So Parlsa started to crotchet and made two more toys so we all had one each, it was great fun.

At the end of the night, Jamie didn't look to well so they all carried him to the sofa and covered him in a blanket, well, actually it is our blanket. Me and Rosie decided that we would lie on our blanket still even though Jamie was poorly.

Everyone else then said bye and went home. They forgot Jamie though, I don't know if they forgot he was on the sofa or what. Dad stayed up a long time checking that Jamie was ok. Me and Rosie also helped by staying on the sofa with him.

Eventually Dad said it was time for bed, I was glad about this. I was so tired, and my mouth felt sore, some of my teeth are feeling very strange at the moment and one of them is moving around quite a bit. I don't know quite what is going on so hopefully my teeth will feel better in the morning.

I went into my crate and cuddled up with Teddy, but I could also see Jamie on the sofa so I kept an eye out to make sure he was ok.

Monday 27th August

I woke Mum up this morning at 7.45am, Jamie was still asleep on the sofa. Mum let us all out for a wee and then started to tidy up all the mess from last night. Mum made Jamie a cup of tea and he looked a lot better than yesterday evening.

Dad got up and then Parsla came and collected Jamie. It was quite a sunny day so Mum put out the blanket on the decking and we all went out and had a sun bathe on it. Mum went to the shops to get dog food and a big picture frame. When she got back she put a very lovely picture in the frame. It was her doggy who died the day after I was born. She said she was hanging it above where he used to sleep. I can see Mum misses him very much so I went out and had cuddles with her on the swing.

In the afternoon, we all started to feel a bit funny, we were all still playing and having fun but we kept making noises from our bums. Mum and Dad said that we all stank. They said that someone must have given us something to eat which we shouldn't have had.

For the rest of the day I played a lot, my gums were very sore and Mum noticed that I had lost my front teeth. She said that I will get nice big ones like Rosie and Maizie have really soon.

Mum and Dad keep laughing when me and Rosie play as we are both so fast. We played for ages and Rosie has taught me so much, like what parts of the body are best to grab if you are trying to catch something.

Later in the evening we all lay in the front room and all three of us started to break wind badly. Mum and Dad said we were all really stinky.

I went for a wee just before bedtime and snuggled up with Teddy again and went to sleep.

Tuesday 28th August

I woke up this morning when Mum came and let me out. I went out for my morning wee and then snuggled on my blanket for a bit.

After breakfast I went out to the garden to go to the toilet and this horrible sound came out of my bottom. I had a really bad runny bum. Luckily though I still felt ok so I got to play a lot with Rosie.

Dad spent time teaching me some commands today again. I'm getting quite good at it, especially as I get treats.

When Mum came home she got a big bucket of hot water and cleaned the grass where I had my poorly bum accidents. After that she started to tidy up the garden, I helped her and I found a scarecrow head in the raspberry bushes that mum was chopping down so I played a lot with it.

Mum tidied up the garden really well and actually made more play space so me and Rosie made the most of that. We ran and played for over an hour. Mum went inside and we followed her and continued to play. Mum kept saying "enough now" but I didn't know what that meant.

Dad came home and laughed that Mum looked to tired out and gave us our tea. I decided after tea to have a power nap. When I woke up, mum had this big long yellow thing, its called a tape measure. She said I was 20 inches tall and a very big boy. I can tell I am getting bigger now as the other dogs don't look massive anymore. I also seem to be getting long hair under my chin which Mum and Dad find really funny.

In the evening we played bitey games for ages and then I settled down to go to bed with Teddy. It was a very busy day.

Wednesday 29th August

This morning I got up at the usual time when mum came and let me out, I went for my morning wee and then snuggled down on the blanket on the floor. Mum went off to work so I decided I would amuse myself by playing with Rosie.

In the afternoon Dad went out. When he came home I got really concerned as he took my crate apart and took it away. I was so worried about this. What was happening?? Well it didn't take long to find out what was happening. I got a new crate, it was massive. I can stretch right out in it. I was so happy. Mum said I need a better blanket in it and said that tomorrow she will go and buy me a nice fluffy one.

When Mum got home I went out into the garden and played with Rosie, we then came in to the house to play, we like playing on the blanket because it is so soft when we fall over. We got really carried away and Mum told us to stop playing as we had been playing for 2 hours. Me and Rosie just ignored her and Mum got a bit cross. She held my collar and said "No". Well, I wasn't happy with this so I tried to play with her by nipping her fingers. Suddenly she told me off with a really loud voice. I got scared and started to cry. Mum let me go and I came up to her and said sorry by licking her face gently. Looks like I got away with it. Mum just can't stay angry at me at all. It's very handy being so cute.

After tea I got myself in a spot of bother, I had gone into the bushes at the bottom of the garden but then discovered I was trapped. Dad came to look for me and found me under the bushes behind the mesh that had been put up to keep me out. He was a bit cross with me but helped me out. He then took me indoors and went out to repair the mesh to stop me going back in there. To be fair, it wasn't that interesting in there.

I went back in and played with mum and Rosie and then dozed on the blanket until it was time to sleep in my new big crate with Teddy.

Thursday 30th August

This morning I got up at the usual time. I didn't bother with a wee though, I just slept on the sofa with Rosie for an hour. Mum went to work and Dad did the usual thing of feeding me and tidying up the house. I played with Rosie for a bit and then Mum came home early.

She had bought some blankets and one was for my crate. It was brilliant, so soft and fluffy. I had a good feel of it and decided I couldn't wait until bed time. Mum got the rope things out again and Maizie and Rosie got really excited, I did too as I realised we were going out. We went up the road and I met lots of people. I didn't really like the cars very much but the other two dogs didn't seem bothered so I guess I just need to man up a bit.

I found lots of twigs in the road so I carried one for quite a distance but I kept dropping it and everyone was getting fed up with me stopping all the time. When we got home we all went out in the garden and dozed in the sun. I Also had a good stretch out on the swing, it was lovely and warm.

Mum and Dad were talking about how big I had got and decided to do another photo of Dad holding me like he did a few weeks ago. They were shocked when they saw how fast I had grown.

I went out to play zoomies with Rosie and Mum was watching, suddenly Rosie stubbed her toe and started to scream, she ran to Mum just like I do and held her paw up for Mum to rub better. Then she just walked off without even a limp.

We went back in and had supper, then I got Teddy and cuddled up in my new crate and new blanket.

Friday 31st August

I woke up at my usual time today and went out for a wee. I came back in and snuggled down on the sofa with Rosie. After breakfast I went outside and played a lot. I also discovered another way to get behind the pond. I basically jumped over the pump and bingo, I was there. I got a ticking off for that by Dad. Dad popped out today and put me in my crate, it was ok as now I have a bigger one I can stretch out.

He wasn't gone for long and he came back with bags of nice stuff, none of which was for me.

When Mum came home, she had done a better job, she had bought a big box of my puppy food and also a big bag of treats, yummy.

After tea, dad went out and Mum played with us a lot. Mum looked a bit sad as her friend had called her and told her she wasn't very well. Me and Rosie decided we would play a lot and try and cheer Mum up. It did seem to work.

41

Mum was very tired so when Dad came home she went to bed. Dad stayed up longer and said that if I had a late wee, that Mum and Dad may get a lay in, ha ha, who are they trying to kid.

After my last wee, I went to bed and cuddled up with Teddy.

Saturday 1st September

This morning I woke mum up at 7am, I raised the alarm in case she was running late. Mum had a day off today as it's the weekend. I had a bit of a play with Rosie and my breakfast and then Mum got out a lead and we left the house. Rosie was not happy that I was going out and started to scream her head off. Dad looked after her and Mum took me out to the car. I hate that thing. Mum had to pick me up to get me in it. Off we went and again it was only a short trip. We were back at the vets.

I got weighed and I am 12.5kg at the moment. Then I decided to sit on the sofa with Mum and wait for Larissa to come and call me. I met some lovely doggies down there, they were all so much bigger than me.

Larrisa called me in and she had a good look at me, she saw my new front teeth and she started to talk to Mum about when my balls go. I didn't understand what they meant. Is she going to just turn up at our house and take all my toys away?

She also told Mum that I am currently half the size I will be once I have grown up, wow, I am going to be a big boy. I'm really looking forward to that.

In the afternoon the sun was shining, so we all went out and sunbathed and played. It was lovely to feel the warmth on my fur.

After tea we stayed out in the garden for ages and played zoomies, I got pretty tired and decided to go indoors, all the others followed me. Dad stayed up late again and then took me out for my night time wee and then I went to bed with Teddy.

Sunday 2nd September

I woke Mum up early again today and she looked really tired. I wasn't though so instead of my usual morning of dozing I decided I wanted to play. Mum tried to stop us but we were so happy playing that we ignored her. Dad then came downstairs and looked really annoyed. He wouldn't even talk to us. Mum said it was because we had woken him up too early.

Mum took our blankets outside and we went outside to play while Dad cooked that lovely Sunday dinner again. I wasn't allowed any of what the other two dogs got but I did have some lovely chicken in with my puppy food.

In the afternoon I half fell in the pond again. I wasn't looking where I was going. It wasn't too bad, I only got a wet foot. I played a lot in the afternoon and Mum took lots of photos of me and Rosie playing.

Mum looked at my teeth because my mouth is sore, she said all my puppy teeth are now falling out. She said she needs to keep an eye on the bottom ones as new teeth are coming through but my puppy teeth are still there.

In the evening we sat out in the garden and enjoyed the sun, Mum and Dad got in the hot tub thing, why they would want to do that I really don't know.

I was so tired today so I was glad to get to bed and snuggle up with Teddy.

Monday 3rd August

I woke up this morning when Mum came down. She got me out of my crate and I went outside. Rosie and Maizie also came and I just wanted to play. Mum told us it was too early but we didn't want to listen to her. Mum gave us all some chews which we ate and it stopped us playing.

After Mum went to work Dad gave us breakfast and then we went out and continued to play in the garden. I am getting so fast on my feet now, it's brilliant. I can now keep up with Rosie when we run down the garden.

Mum got home early and we all went out in the garden and continued to play. Mum noticed when we were playing that my front teeth are pretty big now, my bottom set are really weird at the moment though because my big teeth are coming through but my baby teeth are still there.

In the evening we continued to play on the blanket in the front room and then before we knew it, it was time for bed so I got into my crate and cuddled up with Teddy.

Tuesday 4th August

This morning I got up, went out for a wee and then got told off. Good start to the day and it wasn't even my fault. Rosie had decided that she wanted to play and it was far too early. Mum could see it was Rosie who was trying to play so she decided that Rosie needed to go back into her crate to keep quiet.

This must have really annoyed Rosie because she was pretty annoyed for most of the day.

Dad gave us our breakfast and then started to do the housework. He got out that hoover thing again, I really hate it, and I can see that the other two dogs do too. Well, I decided to be brave, I need to try and save everyone from this nasty creature. It makes so much noise and I really worry that it could try and eat my Dad. I actually ran up to it and started to try and bite it but I am still a bit scared of it. Horrible thing.

When Mum came home, she had bought us lots of big chews, there are three of us and she bought four chews, she said it means there is one spare so we shouldn't squabble over them.

We spent hours playing with our chews and then I had a nap on the sofa, Mum keeps looking in my mouth and checking my teeth, I am getting lots of new big teeth now. When I have all my new big teeth I will be able to kill the hoover in one attack.

Tonight we were all really tired so we all went to bed early and I snuggled down with Teddy.

Wednesday 5th September

I woke up this morning when Mum came and got me. I started to play with Rosie and Mum then made Rosie go back into her crate for a while. Mum got ready for work and then Dad got up.

Dad gave me my breakfast and I went to find my chew that I had been eating yesterday. I spent most of the day trying to make a dent in it, it also made my mouth feel better as at the moment it is very sore still. When Mum came home she looked in my mouth and could see that I have lost more teeth. I now have two massive front teeth and Mum said I look like a rabbit.

I had a jolly good play with Rosie after tea. Maizie tried to join in but Rosie stopped her, she is like my doggie mum and protects me from everything.

In the evening I was pretty tired so I dozed on the blanket and then after my evening wee I went and snuggled down in my crate with Teddy.

Thursday 6th September

This morning I woke up very early, 5.15am to be exact. I wanted Mum to come and get me so I did a few quiet barks, only loud enough for Mum to hear so she could let me out for a wee. Mum really wasn't impressed that I had got her up so early. I decided that after a wee that the best course of action would be to just go to sleep on the sofa until Mum woke up properly.

After Mum went to work Dad gave us breakfast and then I wanted Rosie to play with me but she wouldn't so I just amused myself with my chew. My mouth is very sore and every day I am losing more and more teeth.

Mum came home and I was very happy to see her but she put her computer on and said she was working from home. Me and Rosie were very annoyed at this so we sat right next to her on the sofa and played the bitey game. It was really funny because Rosie kept sticking her feet into Mum's tummy and she was getting annoyed. Mum then put her computer away and went out.

Dad then put me in my crate and Rosie in hers and also went out. I barked a bit to try and stop him and put on a really sad face. He wasn't gone for long and then he came back and let me out. I was very happy.

When Mum got home Dad told her that he was so worried leaving me alone that he had to come home. Mum explained that I need to learn that sometimes I will be in my crate during the day.

I decided it was play time, Rosie was in agreement so we played a lot. It was great fun.

Later on in the evening I had a nice long nap and Mum and Dad took the opportunity to give me lots of cuddles. I was actually quite nice and I felt very loved. Then I just took myself off to bed with Teddy.

Friday 7th August

I woke up this morning when Mum came downstairs, I went out for a wee and tried to play with Rosie so Mum put her back in the crate as she said it was too early to play. Mum noticed I have a lump on my cheek, she had a good feel of it and said that she was going to take me to the vets tomorrow to see Larissa. It isn't bothering me so I don't really see why I need to go.

Mum went off to work as usual and Dad gave me breakfast and then had a battle with the hoover again. I really hate that thing, the noise it makes is terrible.

Later on I had a play with Rosie and then something really weird happened. I went out in the garden and Maizie followed me, I was so surprised with this so I decided to see what she would do if I ran up and down the garden. She actually joined in and played with me. I couldn't believe it, I have been here for two months today and at last she is finally accepting me. I think she was just scared when I first came because I was so small. Well, I am the same size as her now. It was brilliant, I am so happy that she is finally not scared of me. Mum and Dad were really pleased too.

I pretty much played all day and was very tired by the time Mum came home so we all got on the sofa and sat with Mum.

In the evening I was still really tired so I lay on the blanket and cuddled up to Rosie. I really love her, she is so nice to me and has taught me so much. Mum was working out today how old I am, it turns out I am seventeen weeks and 3 days, or 122 days old and Mum said I have now been alive for more than ten million seconds. How very strange. I think I have learnt so much in my 122 days and I think life is pretty much perfect.

Mum and Dad stayed up later tonight, Mum went to bed first and then a bit later Dad took me out for aa wee and I took myself off to bed with Teddy.

Saturday 8th September

I woke up nice and early this morning and had concerns that no one was awake yet so I raised the alarm.

Mum got up and had a tired look about her. She let me out for a wee and then I came in and had a snooze. When Dad got up we were allowed to play so me and Rosie played for a while on the blanket.

I didn't get my breakfast at the usual time, Mum got the lead out and I went out to the car with her. Granny came to the car too. I still don't like getting in the car. We drove for a bit and then I discovered we were back at the vets. It is because I have this lump in my mouth. When I got there Mum put me on the big scales again, I am now 13.5 kilos so I have put on a whole kilo in a week. The girls were all lovely to me and then I went in the room where Larissa usually is. There she was, I really like her. She looked in my mouth but I wouldn't keep still so she left the room. I thought I had done something wrong but she came back with a kong toy and it had a big lump of meat in it. She let me play while she talked with Mum. Then after I finished my kong we left.

I got home and Rosie was there to greet me, we played for most of the day in the garden as it was nice and sunny. After a few hours I got very tired and went indoors to have supper and have a nap.

In the evening Mum and Dad watched a film while we slept on the blanket. Then at the end of the night I went out for my usual wee and cuddled up with Teddy in my crate.

Sunday 9th September

This morning Mum and Dad slept in again so at 7am I thought I had better raise the alarm. Mum got up and let me out of my crate, I went out, did a wee and then settled back to sleep. When Dad got up we had breakfast and Me and Rosie went out to play while they watched tv.

After a while Dad got up and started to cook in the kitchen, the smell was lovely. I have started to recognise that smell, it was chicken. Mum and Dad ate their dinner and then Mum went to tidy up the kitchen and prepare our dinner. I got a whole bowl of chicken all to myself, it was great.

After lunch we all went outside and played, Maizie joined in which was brilliant. She is really starting to like me at last, I mean, what's not to like? We chased the ball around the garden and mum kept pointing this big black thing at me, I think it's called a camera.

In the evening we went back inside as it was getting cold. Mum massaged my face to try and get the lump down a bit, it felt lovely.

Mum and Dad went to bed earlier tonight so I am starting to think that Mum will be going to work tomorrow. We all went out after Mum went to bed, had a wee and then I went straight into my crate and fell asleep with Teddy.

Monday 10th September

Mum came and woke me up this morning so I gathered it was a work day. We all went out for a morning wee and then Rosie had to go back into her crate for an hour because otherwise we play too much and wake up everyone in the street. I went on the sofa and had cuddles with Mum until she went to work. After Mum went to work, Dad did the housework and got out the hoover again. I still really hate that thing. The sun started to shine so Dad put the blankets out so that we could play in the sun. Granny said that we were really spoilt, I don't think she understands that because we are so boney we don't like lying on the hard floor.

Mum came home and started to sort through a load of paperwork so I carried on playing with Rosie. After she finished Mum came and joined us in the garden. We played a lot and chased a ball, it was great fun. I am getting very fast now. I also have a new hobby, Mum feeds the cat and me and Rosie sit and wait for her to finish, this week I have managed to beat Rosie to the dish, I am faster than her now. Rosie seems to know this and cant be bothered to even try now.

In the evening we watched tv and Mum put on Katherine Jenkins, that voice was amazing, I couldn't take my eyes of her, the sound she was making was wonderful. I love her.

Mum went to bed at her usual time and I went out for a wee and came back in and went to my crate to snuggle down with Teddy.

Tuesday 11th September

I woke up at the usual time this morning and headed right out for a wee. Then I got on the sofa to doze while Mum got ready for work. Rosie tried to play again so Mum put her back in the crate as it was too early to play.

After Mum went to work we had breakfast and me and Rosie played again for ages. Then Dad did the housework, out came that hoover again. I am getting braver now as I find that machine so annoying and I worry that Dad may get hurt. The other dogs still run away from it but I am trying to show them that we need to be brave and kill it one day.

When Mum came home we continued to play and it was good fun. I am learning loads of new words, I know that "look, what's this?" means I am going to get something really nice to eat.

I am now getting very tall and Mum says I have a very big head. Mum took another photo of Dad holding me and you can see just how big I am getting. I should be very skinny apparently but I am still quite a chunky puppy.

In the evening, Mum and Dad watched TV for a bit and then we all went off to bed, and I snuggled up with Teddy.

Wednesday 12th September

I woke up a bit later this morning as Mum wasn't going to work. She was home for most of the morning which was lovely and I got to do lots of things like help her have a shower and I licked all the water off her legs when she got out. When she got dressed she had big boots to put on, I wanted to play with them though as they looked like they were nice things to chew.

Mum then went out so Dad did his usual housework with that stupid hoover thing again. He let me have a bit of his toast too, I really liked that it was very tasty.

Mum came back in the afternoon and we all played again. Me and Mum played pully with my string of sausages and it was great. My teeth are getting quite strong now, well, my front ones anyway.

In the evening Mum was so tired that she just fell asleep on the sofa, we realised she must be tired so we all decide to lie down and stay quiet. Mum eventually woke up and went to bed. Dad stayed up for a while and laughed at me when I started yawning really loudly. I was also very tired so I went for a wee and took myself off to my crate and fell asleep with Teddy.

Thursday 13th September

This morning I woke up and had a wee and then I went on the sofa for a cuddle with Mum, I am getting to really enjoy cuddles now, and I love having my head stroked. Mum went off to work and then Dad gave me my breakfast and put our blankets outside so we could play in the sun. I think he did the hoover thing while we were outside so I didn't have to try and attack it.

Mum came home early and did some paperwork which for me was pretty boring. After she finished that she went out in the garden to sort out that big banana plant, she dug one up and put it in a pot and I really tried my best to help with this, Mum was not impressed. So instead I decided to look through the green waste bag and see if there was any sticks I could play with. Mum ended up taking the bag and putting it in the shed, I ran like mad as I saw her open the shed door and I really wanted to have a look inside but Mum saw me coming and quickly shut the door.

After tea, Rosie managed to steal a chew that Dad leaves in my crate, my puppy teeth are rubbish so I never get to eat the chew properly, well Rosie chewed it for ages and then suddenly got up, she looked like she couldn't breath, Mum and Dad went to her and then Mum made her be sick, she was very sick and Mum cleaned it up quickly. It was really scarey because I don't want anything bad to happen to Rosie. Mum and Dad threw all the other chews away and said we wont be having them again.

Rosie went to bed early, I think she was still a bit shocked, so then I went out for a wee and then also went to bed to cuddle Teddy, hoping that Rosie would be back to normal in the morning.

Friday 14th September

Mum woke me up as usual today, I went out for a wee and then settled down on the sofa with Rosie.

Dad got up jus before Mum went to work and then gave me breakfast and then started to do the housework. He got out that hoover thing again, but today I couldn't be bothered to chase it.

I went out and played in the garden for most of the day and enjoyed exploring bits of the garden I don't generally go in.

Mum came home and I was so happy to see her. I started jumping around. It's like I haven't seen her for ages and I miss her a lot when she is at work.

I have also decided that I am really getting to like cuddles now, it took me a while to get it but its brilliant, it makes me feel happy and safe. I really love having the top of my head rubbed.

In the evening Dad went out so I played with Mum and then had a doze. Dad returned quite early and watched tv. Mum went to bed and Dad said he would try and make sure she got a lay in in the morning. Dad kept me up so late, I even thought I could see the sun coming up by the time we went to bed. I was so tired so I went to my crate and snuggled up with Teddy.

Saturday 15th September

I woke up so tired this morning, I only had about 3 hours sleep because Dad kept me up all night. Mum said it worked though as she got an extra hour in bed. It was a lovely dad today, the sun was shining so we all went out into the garden. Mum got a big sack and started to put plants in it, they looked pretty dead to be fair so I think she was just trying to make the garden look nice. I really decided I needed to help Mum so as she was putting the dead stuff into the bag I was taking it all out and sorting through it to see if there was anything interesting in there. Mum got a little bit fed up with me helping. After Mum finished the garden we had a good play on the blanket and sunbathed.

Mum weighed me again today, she is struggling to pick me up now. Today I am 14 and a bit kilos so I am getting bigger every day.

In the evening, Mum bought the blanket back in and we all played on it and enjoyed eating chews. I went out and had a wee and went to bed a lot earlier as I was so tired. So I snuggled down with Teddy and went to sleep right away.

Sunday 16th September

52

I woke up and alerted Mum that she had overslept, I still can't work out her routine so I always wake her up if she isn't awake by 7am. Mum made herself a cup of coffee and then went and sat on the sofa. I joined her as I wanted a cuddle. Rosie also came up and joined us. When Dad got up he made a cup of tea, drank it and then went to the kitchen and started to cook Sunday dinner. Now, I am getting the hang of that. I love the smells that it makes. We always have to wait though, so Mum does the dishes and then we get our roast. I wish I was big though as the other dogs get a massive dinner and I just get a bit of chicken in with my puppy food.

In the afternoon we all played on our blanket and Rosie found my chew. I can't ever make a dent in it as my puppy teeth are too small, but Rosie didn't have a problem chewing it. We also had a doze as we were all so full of roast dinner.

In the evening Rosie continued eating that chew, she then suddenly got up and looked very odd. Dad said to Mum that she looked like she was choking. Mum grabbed her and started rubbing her chest, Rosie was suddenly very sick. There were big chunks of chew in it. Mum and dad searched around to make sure there were no more chews lying around. I was so frightened because Rosie looked quite poorly.

The rest of the evening was quiet. Rosie didn't want to play so we cuddled up until bed time when I went into my crate and cuddled up with Teddy.

Monday 17th September

This morning Mum woke me up and let me out of my crate, I ran straight over to check Rosie was ok. She was fine. I was very happy to see her back to normal so I gave her a big cuddle on the sofa. After Mum went to work, Dad took us all out for a walk, he said he is very proud of me as I walk well on the lead. I love being in the middle of the other two dogs, I feel safe. I am still not keen on all the cars though, I get a bit worried.

The weather is not as nice anymore, I liked it better when I was really small because it was always sunny. Dad went in the garden and took down the cover of the gazebo, apparently there is going to be a storm. I have never seen a storm so I hope it isn't too scarey like when the wind blew over the big gazebo that time.

Mum came home and had some new dog treats for us, she said they were much safer and that we wouldn't get those hide chews anymore. That's a shame as I did quite like them.

In the evening me and Rosie got up with Mum and all cuddled up together until bedtime. So before bed I went and inspected the garden and then had a wee and cuddled up in my crate with Teddy.

Tuesday 18th September

This morning Mum overslept again. Well, that's what I thought. It turned out she had a day off work. We all sat on the sofa for cuddles and then Dad got the hoover out. I was really concerned as he took ages to hoover, I obviously got cross with it so I kept attacking it. After Dad finished I was horrified, he bought down an even bigger hoover. Mum filled it with water, it was so loud, I really didn't like it so I went outside. It was cold outside so I buried myself in the blanket, but it was no good. I really needed to go back inside. Mum had moved the table and my crate, what was going on I asked myself? The carpet seemed wet as well. It was awful.

It turned out that Mum had decided that because I was now fully housetrained that she would clean all the carpet downstairs so it is nice and clean for winter and also for something called Christmas. I don't know what Christmas is but Dad seems quite excited by it.

When Mum eventually finished with the cleaner she put the room back to normal and we all got on the sofa, leaving her a tiny space to sit on. She checked my teeth again, all my front ones are now big but my fangs are still puppy ones. I can't wait until all my big teeth are here, it will be much better for playing and eating.

In the evening we all got on the sofa again because the floor was still damp. I stayed up there until bedtime and then went for my usual garden patrol and then went to my crate and snuggled up with Teddy for the night.

Wednesday 19th September

I woke up this morning and after my wee I settled down on the sofa. The carpet is still a bit damp but to be fair it looks really nice and clean now. Mum went off to work and Dad gave us our food and then did the housework. I didn't bother with the hoover today as I now just have my mind set on killing the awful one that made everything wet.

Dad got a parcel in the afternoon, but didn't open it until we returned from our walk, It was another big soft blanket for us. It is brand new and very snuggly, I like it a lot. I tried really hard to make myself a bed with it but I really don't know what I am doing. I seem to end up with a big mound of blanket rather than a nice dog bed like Rosie makes.

Mum came home and I played a lot more, I like it when she get home. Mum says I go wild as I like doing zoomies. I am getting really good at them.

After tea I snuggled on my blanket mound and dozed all evening. It had been such a busy day that I was glad to go to bed with Teddy at the end of the day.

Thursday 20th September

I woke up and went out for a wee, when I came back I went on the sofa and cuddled up with Mum until she got ready to go to work. Rosie seemed quiet today, I don't think she quite felt her usual self and had no interest in playing with me today. I was getting a bit bored to be fair.

After breakfast I tried again to play with Rosie but she still didn't want to so I just got a few toys together and amused myself. Dad got the hoover thing out again so I practiced my attacking skills on that. I really hate it.

Dad had to go out in the afternoon so I went to sleep in my crate while he was gone, he didn't go out for long though so I wasn't too annoyed.

When Mum came back I get really hyper again, Rosie did too so we played a lot. It was horrible weather today so we just played indoors. After Rosie had enough I decided to play zoomies and practice my target aim, so I ran like mad through the kitchen which is really slippy so I would run and take a while to get anywhere, once I hit the dining room carpet it was all systems go. I zoomed right through the dining room and then lifted off the floor and landed on Mum. Mum laughed and I took one big leap off her and landed on Dad. They said I was like a little devil. Eventually I calmed down and sneakily found a half eaten chew that Mum and Dad obviously didn't see when they threw them all away.

Mum spotted me eating it and said she needed to get it off my, I hid the whole piece in my mouth. Mum grabbed my mouth and put her fingers right in, I was not happy with this so I growled at her. I shouldn't have done that because she told me off. I decided the best course of action was to just let her take the chew. So then I just gave up and went and dozed off on the sofa.

I was quite tired so off I went to my crate to cuddle up with Teddy. I hadn't been in bed long and I was awoken with a pain in my tummy, I have had this before so I had to raise the alarm. Mum came down and asked if I wanted the toilet, I just looked at her and didn't want to move really so she went back to bed. About five minutes later I knew I really needed the loo so I called out again. Dad came and let me out and took me to the garden. I had a very upset tummy. I really didn't sleep a lot as every half hour through the night I needed to wake Mum and Dad up to take me out to the garden. I really hope I feel better tomorrow.

Friday 21st September

 Well, after an awful night of being poorly, Mum stayed with me from 5am and gave me some medicine. I was feeling a little bit better but thought I would just make the most of the situation, so I got up on the sofa with her and had a cuddle. Mum went to work and it was business as usual, housework, that blimin awful hoover and a good play in the sun. It was quite a nice day but it isn't like when I was little anymore, it feels cold even in the sun.

When Mum got home we all played together, It was great fun and I was feeling so much better than I did last night. Something weir did happen
56

though, I was playing with a toy in the dining room, I heard Mum call me so I went over. She started to laugh and told Dad that she only called me with her mind and not her voice. She said it means we are getting in tune whatever that means.

To be fair, there wasn't really much else to report on today because I was so tired after my night being poorly that I slept for most of the evening and then went to my crate early to cuddle up with Teddy.

Saturday 22nd September

This morning I woke up feeling magnificent. I was so much better and don't have a tummy ache anymore. Mum put me on the scales again today, I am now 15.3 kilos. Mum said that's quite big for a puppy.

It rained all day today and I didn't really want to go out in the garden and get wet, apart from when I need the loo. I was in a very impish mood today and wanted to play all day. I did epic zoomies around the house and annoyed Mum I think.

Dad went out in the afternoon and left us too it so Mum decided to watch a film, there was lots of weird screaming in it, it was what you would call a horror movie, I wasn't keen. Mum gave us some tea and then made hers, well, her's was rubbish, I think Dad is the only one who makes nice food in the house.

After tea Mum tried to watch tv but me and Rosie were playing lots and she kept saying she couldn't hear the tv over us. In the end (after about three hours) she told us we had to stop and settle down. She wanted to watch another film. Mum stayed up a lot longer than she usually would and we were all concerned when it was time for bed because Dad still wasn't home.

Mum took me out for a wee last thing and then settled us all down for bed. I went in my crate and cuddled into Teddy hoping that Dad would be back soon.

Sunday 23rd September

57

I woke up at around 7.30am, and there was still no Dad and Mum was in bed. I raised the alarm to get her to come downstairs and within a minute, there she was. I went out for a very quick wee as it was still raining and then came back inside. Mum gave us all breakfast and then we started to play. Rosie wasn't overly keen to start with, I think it's because on a Sunday they all have this weird not wanting to do anything day. Well, I wans't even going to entertain that so I wanted to play and indeed I did.

Later in the morning it stopped raining, I went outside with Mum and then we heard Rosie barking, I came back inside and who was stood there?? Dad, that's who. I was so happy, I ran up and jumped all over him. He was happy to see me too. I could tell.

Dad had a cup of tea and then started to cook Sunday roast, Rosie and Mum got on the sofa and watched their usual Sunday morning programme. There isn't even any dogs on it. Our roast was lovely again, although I still only get the chicken in with my puppy food and don't get any veg. I want to grow faster so I can eat the same as them

After dinner no one wanted to play with me at all so I went out in the garden to explore. I managed to dig a nice hole in the empty tortoise run. I see Dad put some pots in there to try and stop me, yeah, like that's going to work. There is also a shed thing down there with shelves but no door, I had a really good look to see what I could find, but everything was boring.

I came back in and had my tea and then decided to have a snooze on the rug for a bit. While I was snoozing I could hear Mum and Dad talking about me, they were saying that I was starting to get hairy and my legs look like a dog they had a long time ago called Tramp. They seem very happy about this so all was good. At around 10.30 we all went out and had a wee and then I went into my crate and cuddled up with Teddy to go to sleep.

Monday 25th September

I woke up this morning when Mum came downstairs but I really didn't want to get up and neither did Rosie, but we were all told by Mum that we should go out for a wee.

We came back in and dozed on the sofa because we know that if we start playing at that time of day we will get a telling off. Mum went to work and Dad did the housework and then took us out for a walk. I always walk in the middle of the other two, it makes me feel safe. It's really funny because Rosie always has two poohs when we go for a walk and she always does it in the middle of driveways which gets on Dad's nerves a bit, he always picks it up but it's always in a drive way entrance.

When we got home the other dogs wanted to go to sleep but I really wanted to play after the excitement of my walk.

Mum came home and I explained to her that I really wanted to play so she went and found the special blue ball. I love that ball and when I have it the other two dogs chase me up and down the garden. It's great that she is starting to play with me more. When we all got tired we went and crashed out in the front room. I stretched out on the sofa and the girls lay on the blankets on the floor.

We all lounged around for the rest of the evening and then went out for our wee before settling down in my crate with Teddy.

Tuesday 25th September

I got up this morning when Mum woke me up and went out for a wee. It was really cold out there this morning so I came back in and snuggled down on the blanket.

When Dad got up he didn't look too well, Mum went to work and then dad did the housework. He still didn't look well and looked really cold. I tried to amuse myself by playing with Rosie.

The sun came out and it was quite warm so we went out and played again, I got into so much trouble with Dad though. So what happened was I was out playing and I misjudged where I was going, I was trying to jump over the ferns to get to the back of the pond as Dad had blocked the way I usually got there, but I didn't make it and I full on fell in the pond, it is really deep, I managed to get myself out and then thought I had better go in as I was really cold. I came in through the dog flap and Dad saw me. He wasn't happy and made me stay outside. He had to fix all the netting over the pond too as it sank when I fell in.

Dad still wasn't feeling well so I suppose my accident just made him feel worse. Mum came home and saw that Dad wasn't well. She played with me to keep me amused and then cooked tea for Dad too.

After tea, me and Rosie played for ages again and then we all curled up on the blanket until bed time. I was happy to get in my crate and cuddle up with teddy tonight.

Wednesday 26th September

I woke up this morning and didn't want to get out of bed. I was very snug in my new blanket. I eventually got up and went to snuggle with Mum on the sofa. Dad got up and looked a lot better than he did yesterday. Dad started to hoover and so I decided to risk my chances and see if Maizie fancied a play. I couldn't believe it, she lay on the floor and showed me her tummy, it was great, the beast was being nice. We played for ages and I think Rosie enjoyed having a break. After Dad finished hoovering me and Maizie went outside and continued to play. I am so happy now, this means I have finally be accepted by her. I could jump for joy!!!

Dad told mum all about me and Maizie today, she said that they see me as top dog now and that I am bigger they are happy to treat me like they did with Zak, their friend who died in May.

In the evening Rosie decided she would play with me so we both sat on Mum's lap and played the bitey game, Mum got annoyed and told us to play on the floor as she didn't want her nose broken again. We played for ages and then we went out for an evening wee and I went into my crate and cuddled up with Teddy. It was a really good day today.

Thursday 27th September

I got up this morning, it is starting to get a bit cold in the morning now. I managed to hold out for a morning wee for quite a while. Eventually I had to give in and go for it. I rushed back in and snuggled on the sofa for a while. Me and Rosie have now learnt that if we play before 8am we get in trouble.

Mum went to work and Dad did his usual chores. I still haven't managed to kill that hoover though. I played with Maizie and Rosie a lot today and we had good fun.

I am at the point now where I am getting really fed up with having some big teeth and some puppy teeth. My puppy fangs look a bit silly now, I wish my big ones would hurry up. Also my beard at the moment according to Mum and Dad looks like a shoe brush. I think that's a bit unfair really, and I hope it starts growing down soon instead of sticking out everywhere. I am now taller than the other dogs and also the heaviest, and my feet are still looking massive.

When Mum got home she tidied up the garden a bit while we all played, I take the blue ball and run up and down the garden with it and the others follow me. Poor Rosie and Maizie get tired way before I do.

I did manage to get Maizie to have another play with me, It was really weird because Mum started to cry, Dad asked her what was wrong and she said she was just happy that Rosie and Maizie have both accepted me now and treat me like they used to treat Zak, but Mum said she still missed him and felt like she was the only one now that still misses him. He sounds like he was a really cool dog and I know mum still misses him, but I know that she really loves me too and that slowly she will be happy again. I will make sure of that.

After tea, I played and snoozed, I also watched a bit of that tv thing, sometimes there are really good pictures on it and I like some of the noises it makes too. After a pretty nice and chilled out evening I did my bed time wee and then went and snuggled with Teddy in my crate.

Friday 28th September

Today I didn't really want to get up again, my crate with all those blankets and Teddy is so cozy. Eventually I got up and went out into the garden. It was a usual run of the mill day, I played and dozed, I also tried to kill the hoover again, but I just can't do it. I think I need to get a bit bigger and then I will finally get it.

In the afternoon, Dad took the blankets outside so we all sunbathed and enjoyed the warmth of the sun. Mum came home and we all went wild, we ran and played in the garden, it's really funny because when we get going Mum and Dad get scared that we are going to run into them so they move out of the way.

Everyone went indoors when the sun went from the garden. I thought I would have another attempt at getting to the back of the pond. I didn't make it but this time I managed to save myself from a swim and only got my front paws wet. I will get to the back of the pond one day. I will bide my time and wait until Mum and Dad think I am sensible as they are bound to take the fence down that stops me getting there.

After tea, Mum had a bath, I love bath time, we all stand resting our heads on the edge of the bath, I love licking the bubbles from the bath and drinking the warm water. Mum got a load of the bubbles and put them on my head, I think I must have looked really silly.

In the evening Dad went out so we all crashed out on the sofa, Rosie and Maizie were way too tired to want to play so we chilled out and dozed for the rest of the evening.

Dad came home later in the evening and gave me my supper and then I decided to turn in early so I went to bed and cuddled up with Teddy.

Saturday 29th September

I woke Mum up at 7.15 this morning as I thought again she could be late for work. Mum made herself a coffee and after my wee I went and joined her on the sofa. When it got a bit warmer Mum took our blankets out so we had somewhere soft to play. I played for quite awhile and then I decided I would help Mum with her gardening. She was chopping branches and putting the bits she cut off into a bag. I had to have a look and see if there were any branches in there that would be fun to play with. The bag was just full of little twigs and they were far to boring to play with. I ended up getting my ball and just getting the other two dogs to chase me.

We didn't really do that much today, I got weighed again. Today I was 15.6kg, so I haven't grown much this week but I have still grown a little bit.

In the evening we all settled down to watch the tv and Mum said she had to go to bed early as we all are due to have a busy day tomorrow. I don't know what she has planned but I think it includes me. I went out and had a wee and then went in to my crate and cuddles up with Teddy to dream about what is going to happen tomorrow.

Sunday 30th September

Mum woke me up this morning and started to get ready really early, I was confused as usually Sunday is a chill out day watching soaps in the morning. Dad got up and took us all out in the garden and then Mum was messing around with stuff in the cupboard, when we came back in I noticed that the harnesses were out. Mum put her coat on and then put harnesses on to me and Rosie, she then took us out to the car, Mazie stayed with Dad.   We got in the car and started to drive. Mum stopped the car after a little while and then got out and went to this tv screen in the wall of a shop. Suddenly there was a loud noise, the car alarm was going off, Mum turned it off and laughed and said it was because we had moved. So we carried on driving for quite a long way, the road ended up getting smaller and smaller and then suddenly Mum left the road and started to drive in a field.

Mum stopped the car and undid our harnesses, we got out and all I could see was lots of people with lots of dogs. There was so much to see, Mum walked up to a lady and gave her a hug, she also said hello to Me and Rosie. Then she went up to a man and they hugged and he also said hello.

It was really interesting, there were people walking their dogs around a ring, then someone would go up to each dog and feel every part of them, I was so interested and loved watching, So did Rosie and at one point she wanted a better view and managed to jump onto the bonnet of the big land rover we were stood by. Mum lifted her off and said she wasn't allowed to do that. We went over to look at collars to keep Rosie amused and Mum bought her a nice new purple one.

Mum's friend Banf took me for a walk and I ended up standing where those other people had been, it was all a bit odd, I could hear Rosie shouting at me and the next thing I knew, there she was. Mum came and got her and then I was left with Banf again. This lady came up and starting looking in my mouth and ears, then she stroked me. She didn't look like a vet but I felt like I was being examined, at one point she even squeezed my little nutlets. I have to say though, I did rather like that.

The lady gave Banf a blue rosette, apparently I was the 2nd best puppy there. I felt so proud and Mum was smiling and saying Dad would be very happy. We came back to Mum and Rosie was very glad I was back. I also had started to get very hungry, all was good though because one of Bamf's friends gave us a big bit of sausage roll. A bit later, Mum hugged everyone goodbye and then we walked back to the car, Banf and Mum said goodbye and we got back into the car with our harnesses on. We were so tired we both fell asleep.

We woke up when we realised the car had stopped, we were home. We both ran in and said hello to Maizie, Mum gave Dad my rosette and he was really happy, Mum kept calling me a show pony. As soon as we settled, Dad gave us dinner, I was so hungry and wolfed my food right down. I then went and snuggled up on my blanket and pretty much stayed there until it was time to go to bed. Today was my first time of staying out all day. I think it will take time to get used to that.

I had a very early night today, I went out for a wee and then snuggled up to sleep with Teddy and dreamed about all the new things I had seen today.

Monday 1st October

I really didn't want to get up this morning, I was so tired from yesterday. Mum opened the crate and I just decided to stay in bed as long as my bladder would hold out. Eventually I went out for a wee and then I went and lay on the sofa. Mum went to work and then Dad gave me breakfast. I was still really hungry from everything I did yesterday. Dad got the hoover out again and I really couldn't be bothered to chase it today. I decided that in the afternoon the best idea would be to catch up on some sleep.

Mum came home and I woke up and started to play with Rosie, Maizie joined in so we ran up and down the garden for ages. We came back in when we heard Dad cooking tea. After Mum and Dad had their tea we had ours. I eat my tea really quickly, I can eat the whole lot in under 10 seconds. Well, I wouldn't want anyone else to get it would I?

We all settled down for the evening and dozed on our big blanket and then Mum and Dad woke us up so we could go out for our wee before bed. I then went into my crate and snuggled up with Teddy.

Tuesday 2nd October

I got up eventually this morning after Mum had made her cup of tea, I went out and had a quick wee and came back in and settled down on the sofa. I don't like it in the mornings now as it is still dark when we get up. I really don't understand what is going on.

After Mum went to work, Dad got the leads out and took us for a walk, it was the longest walk I had ever been on, we went to the end of the road we usually go down and then to my shock, we carried on going. We went past a really stinky place, it smelled just like poohs that people do, it did get better though because we walked through a lane and ended up in a nice big garden with fields all around it. Rosie looked fed up, Dad said she only likes short walks but I need to build on making my bones nice and strong.

65

We eventually got home and I had my dinner and then went to sleep. I was very tired. I woke up a few hours later when Mum got home and we played with my ball. It's a great game, I take the ball and run up and down the garden and the other two dogs chase me all the time.

I did get into a spot of bother though as I discovered that under the pretend grass there is a piece of garden that is perfect for digging a big hole. Dad found the hole and told me off and put a big pot over it so I had my fun totally ruined.

In the evening we all went and sat in the front room and we dozed. I slept with my legs over Rosie's head, she makes a brilliant foot stool I decided. At the end of the night I went outside and then came back in to snuggle up with Teddy again. I slept very well as I was so tired.

Thursday 4ᵗʰ October

I didn't want to get up again this morning, but eventually I did and then cuddled up with Mum on the sofa until she went to work. Dad gave me breakfast and then after that he started doing the housework. On the window sill I found a small glass thing in a little case so I decided to take it to my bed and investigate it further. Dad looked in to see what I was doing so I picked up my bone and started to chew that so he wouldn't see I had stolen anything. After he went away I got the glass thing and then I gave it a good chew. It was very crunchy and I managed to get it out of the case.

Dad came over and saw what I had done and looked very worried, He picked all the glass up and then made a phone call. When Dad put the phone down he put me on the lead and took me out in the car.

When the car stopped I realised I was at the vets, perhaps it was time for her to look at me again. She checked me over, looked in my mouth and felt my tummy. I was so happy to see Larissa though, I do really like her. I was really pleased that I didn't have any needles stuck in me, Larrisa told Dad to keep an eye on my pooh and to bring me back if I get poorly. It turns out what I ate was a glass nail file.

I got home and then Mum came home. Dad told her what had happened today, and she told me I was very silly. I was ok though and I feel very well. Mum and Dad had tea and then gave us ours. I ate mine really quickly again and then I really wanted to eat he other dog's tea. Dad lifted up their bowls when they had finished and and put them on the kitchen worktop. I worked out I could reach so I started to help myself. Dad came and told me off, apparently what I was doing is called counter surfing and it is seen as very naughty for dogs to do that.

Later in the evening I went and slept on the blanket with Rosie until bedtime again, then I went out for a wee and snuggled down in my crate with Teddy. Dad said he hoped I had a good night sleep.

Friday 5th October

I got up this morning and decided to stay in bed for a bit. It is really quite chilly in the morning now. I eventually got out of bed, had a big stretch and then went out for a wee. I then came in and snuggled up to Mum while she drank her morning coffee.

After Mum went to work, Dad took us for a nice walk, I just find the outside world fascinating and like looking at everything and saying hello to everyone. When we got home I was tired for a little bit so I had a snooze and then I decided to go out and see what I could find to do in the garden.

I discovered at the bottom of the garden I could lift up the fake grass and when I did I found a patch of ground that was perfect for hole digging. I was really impressed with the hole I dug, so when Dad saw it and got cross I couldn't understand why. He covered it over and then called me to come indoors.

Mum came home and we all got really excited, we played for ages and Mum decided to stay out of our way and let us get on with it. I played with Rosie and Maizie as they took it in turns to play. It was great.

In the evening we all settled down on the blanket until bedtime and I had an evening wee and then went to bed and snuggled up with Teddy.

Saturday 6th October

The weather wasn't great when I got up this morning, it looked like it was going to rain. Mum wasn't feeling very good this morning so we decided to be quiet and leave her to get better. Dad decided to take us out before the rain came. We went on a nice long walk again and I met some lovely people and some very friendly dogs. I like meeting new dogs, I tend to lie down on my back so they can see I am friendly.

When we returned home, we all settled down and had a very lazy day as Mum still looked unwell. We really didn't do much today after that apart from eat and sleep.

In the evening we all cuddled up together and then later I went off for a wee and then went to bed to snuggle up with Teddy.

Sunday 7th October

I didn't wake up Mum today, one of the tortoises did instead. I didn't really want to get up this morning. Mum looked a lot better today so we were all happy, today is also that day where we get our special lunch, I love it. Mum weighed me today and I am 16.3kilos, Dad decided to feed me a bit more as my brother is a kilo heavier than me. Mum found my brother and sister on facebook and they are keeping in touch and swapping photos of us all.

After lunch we played a lot in the garden, I have this blue ball which, when I pick it up, the other two dogs chase me. I love this game and I think they do too. We played this game until Rosie and Maizie got really tired and then we decided to all crash out on the blanket and play gently. My mouth got full of blood at one point, it was really weird, Mum had a look and could see I had lost another puppy tooth. I have lost most of them now, but still have a few fangs. At one point Mum said I sounded like I was crunching something and then she laughed as I spat out yet another tooth.

I like Sunday's, I enjoy being home with Mum and Dad all day and I really like the way we all do things together. I am learning as well that it is nice to have a lazy day once a week.

In the evening we all had an early night and I went and snuggled up in bed with Teddy.

Monday 8th October

This morning Mum woke me up, I lay in bed for a little while as I was comfy and didn't really want to get up. I eventually went out to the loo and then came back in and sat in Mum's place on the sofa. She had to perch on the edge. When she went to work I had breakfast and then I decided to play a lot and try and practice my zoomies. I think I did Dad's head in as he was trying to get on with his housework. I stopped so I could try and fight the hoover again, but I'm still not managing to win the fight.

In the late afternoon when Mum came home we all started to play again. Mum got in the hot tub and I was really fascinated as there was lots of mist around it. I think she is a bit mad really because I think it would be too cold to be outside in water now, I don't even go near the pond anymore for that very reason.

When Mum got out of the hot tub we all went indoors and settled down on the blankets until it was time to go to bed. I took myself off outside just before bedtime to do my last wee of the evening and then settled into bed with Teddy.

Tuesday 9th October

I was woken by Mum this morning and I didn't want to get up so I stayed in bed for a bit longer. I eventually got up and then snuggled up with Rosie on the sofa. Mum got ready for work and went off as usual.

Dad gave us breakfast and then did the housework, that hoover came out again, today I decided I would try and kill it, but I am still not big enough.

It was quite a sunny day so I entertained myself by making the other two dogs chase me as I had the special blue ball that everyone likes. We ran for ages and then when we got tired we all crashed out on the blankets in the sun.

Mum came home early today and came and sat out with us. We managed to get more energy to play. Later on that evening Mum got in the hot tub again, it was cold and the mist was coming off the water. She didn't stay in it as she said she was too hot so when she got out I went and cuddled up with her on the sofa as she still felt really warm. Mum said she really likes it now I am out of the bitey puppy stage and that I am starting to get really cuddly. Well of course I am, I love being nice to everyone, well, maybe not the cat as she can still be really nasty to me.

We all went to bed pretty early tonight so I popped out for a quick wee and then went to bed to cuddle up with Teddy.

Wednesday 10th October

Today I had a lay in. I eventually got up and went on the sofa, Dad got up and pretty much went right out, he had to go and see the human vet he said. When he got back, Mum put me on the lead and took me out in the car. I still hate getting in it so Mum has to lift me in. When we parked up we went into a familiar building, it was where Mum works. I went in and was really excited to see Sarah and Marie, they said I am getting big. Marie came and gave me a cuddle, I was so excited I managed to undo her buttons on her shirt. Ooops! I really enjoyed seeing Marie and Sarah and before I knew it we were back off in the car. I again insisted on being lifted into the car, Mum says I need to learn to get in the car myself now as I am getting to heavy to carry.

When we got home the other two dogs were happy to see me. I think they thought I had been to the vet. We went outside and Mum took out our blankets so we could all sunbathe in the garden. It was really hot so we went from blanket to shady swing seat and alternated when we got too hot or cold.

In the evening Mum went out to the hot tub again and this time she took this little black thing with her. She turned it on and music came out. I couldn't work out how that was happening so I picked it up to inspect it. Mum told me too put it back down again so I did.

Mum came back in and I cuddled up with her again as she was so nice and warm. I was pretty tired after today so I decided to have an early night and snuggle up with Teddy.

Thursday 11th October

I woke up this morning and decided to stay in my crate for a bit, I was nice and snug and it was all dark outside. I ended up getting up and going for a wee because I wanted to cuddle up to Mum on the sofa. Mum got ready for work and then went, Dad gave me my breakfast and I went back to sleep for a while.

After Dad did the house work I played with Maizie, Rosie wasn't really in the mood. Maizie is now getting really friendly with me and I am starting to trust her more now as she no longer looks angry that I live here too.

When Mum came home we continued to play, Maizie and Rosie took it in turns to play with me. It was great fun and I really love playing with them both now. Mum reached down on to the carpet and found one of my teeth, it was the last one to fall out so I now no longer have any puppy teeth left. Mum put my tooth in a pot with the others that she has found.

In the evening we all snuggled up on the blanket until bedtime and then I went out for my night time wee and then went into my crate and snuggled up with Teddy.

Friday 12th October

I got up early with Mum today and went out for a morning wee. I then went and snuggled on the sofa with Mum and Rosie. Mum left as usual for work and Dad gave me my breakfast and tried to do the housework. Dad has not been well and has a really bad cough at the moment.

He couldn't even take us for a walk today so I managed to exercise everyone by running around with the blue ball in my mouth. I managed to keep the other two dogs running about for ages, but eventually they got tired and went to sleep.

Mum came home a bit earlier today so we played loads, she keeps checking my mouth as well to see that my teeth are all growing as they should. I am starting to look a little bit scruffy too Mum says, I thought that would mean I was in trouble but apparently Mum seems to think scruffy is a good thing.

In the evening we all chilled out in the front room and Mum and Dad watched tv. Bed time was a little bit odd tonight, Mum went up to bed and Dad slept down with us, he said he didn't want to keep Mum awake all night coughing. So instead of Teddy I cuddled up with Dad tonight.

Saturday 13ᵗʰ October

I woke up this morning still cuddled up with Dad, he was still poorly. Mum came down and made herself a coffee. I got on the sofa and cuddled up with Mum, Rosie came and joined us too.

Just before breakfast, Mum weighed me again. I am now 17kg. I am getting to be a big boy and am now way taller than the other two dogs.

It rained really hard today and we didn't want to go out and get wet so today we decided that the best plan of action was to practice zoomies around the house. I loved it, Mum and Dad however, looked pretty scared. They say they think I may run into them and get hurt. I wouldn't do that though as I am now able to forward plan and work out where I am going to end up when I run fast.

In the evening, we were supposed to have visitors but we had to cancel as Dad really wasn't feeling well and didn't want to pass anything on to anyone else. So instead we all snuggled down on the blankets and stayed there pretty much all night as Dad slept downstairs again.

Sunday 14ᵗʰ October

Mum came down this morning and made herself and Dad a cup of tea and coffee. Dad was still coughing all night and looked very tired this morning. After breakfast Dad started to cook lunch, I got excited as I saw dad put a whole chicken in the oven instead of just a leg. After a while there was a knock at the door, it was a man, apparently he is called grandad, he is dad's dad. He came and said hello to me, he seemed like a very nice man. Not long after, Granny came in too. They all sat at the table and had a big dinner, it was lovely with all the smells going on. I really hoped that we got to have the leftovers.

Mum cleared the table and did the dishes, then to my excitement we got a big bowl of chicken each. It was really tasty. After Granny and Grandad left we all went and lay down in the front room, we had very full tummies and all just wanted to sleep. Apparently while we were all asleep Mum took a video of us all asleep, Dad was also asleep.

We all woke up and had supper, it was funny because we then all felt full and fat again. We watched tv and then later in the evening we watched Dad set up his bed on the front room floor again and Mum went up to bed. I curled up and went to sleep on the blanket with Dad.

Monday 15th October

I stayed on the blanket with Dad when Mum got up this morning. Dad had slept on the floor with us again last night because he has such a bad cough at the moment. After Mum went to work, Dad tidied up a bit and then sat back down in his chair. I don't like it when Dad isn't very well. Neither do the other two dogs. I tried to play with Rosie but she wasn't very keen today. Then I started to play with Maizie, for a while it was fun and then I must have bitten Maizie a bit too hard. She was really angry and tried to bite me. I got really scared and ran into the front room screaming. Dad gave me a hug and then told Maizie off. I must have bitten her a bit hard, that's all I can think of, she knows I wouldn't be nasty to her.

Mum came back early, she had been to university apparently, she is doing some testing thing involving stretching her back. I know she gets back ache so perhaps it will make her better. We are all excited when Mum came home and me and Rosie had a good play. I love playing with Rosie as she doesn't get cross with me very often. Later on that evening, Maizie told me off again, I don't know what is up with her today, she is very moody. I suppose she could just be tired with not sleeping properly because of Dad coughing.

In the evening we all slept on the blankets with Dad again, I really hope that he feels better tomorrow and that Maizie is in a better mood. Today was a really rubbish day.

Tuesday 16th October

Today I woke up lying on the blanket that Dad was sleeping under. Rosie was also there too. Mum came down and suggested that Dad went to bed for a bit. I went out to the loo and then I came back in and snuggled up on the sofa with Rosie. Dad got back up again and looked really awful and couldn't stop coughing, it did get a bit annoying but we all felt so sorry for him. Maizie was in a much better mood today. I think we are all just a bit tired because Dad is ill.

Mum went to work and Dad gave me breakfast, I played for a little bit but was still tired so I was pretty happy to go in my crate for a bit while Dad went to the doctors. When he came back me and Rosie had a little play but didn't really feel like it so we all just snuggled in with Dad for the afternoon.

When Mum came home we all got excited and started to play, I played tug of war with Rosie and that seemed to cheer her up a lot. I also played with Mum, I thinks she only wanted to play so she could look in my mouth and check all my teeth are growing properly. We ended up all chilling out in the front room until bedtime and then I went out for a wee and tonight I went back in my crate to cuddle Teddy.

Wednesday 17th October

Mum came down this morning and told Dad to go back to bed as he had been sleeping on the sofa again due to his nasty cough. I just went right up on the sofa as I was tired from not being able to sleep properly. Dad came down again just before Mum went to work and after Mum had gone, Dad gave us breakfast. We all went out in the garden and had a good play and tired ourselves out. We played on and off for most of the day and Dad did housework and other stuff.

Seeing my day was pretty regular I can take this opportunity to talk about one of my biggest achievements. I have learned how to make sure I get any left over cat food first. Apparently this was a competition that Rosie and Zak had going on. Until Zak started to get poorly he was always the winner but then as he got slower Rosie would always beat him to it. Well, I have become the master of this now. I sit and wait in the kitchen and then as soon as the cat lifts her head out of the bowl I leg it and get to the dish. Rosie would try and beat me but has now given in. It's fab but I don't often get anything as the cat usually eats all her food.

Anyway back to today, Mum came home a bit earlier and we all got really excited and started to play. Mum also played with me for ages and we played bitey games mixed in with some learning. I am so good at sit and lay down now that Mum says she is going to teach me some fun stuff too.

In the evening we all curled up on the big blanket until it was time to go to bed. I then went to bed and cuddled up with Teddy.

Thursday 18th October

I got up this morning after sleeping with Dad, he went up to bed wen Mum came down. I was in such a cuddly mood this morning so I gave Mum loads of cuddles before work. Dad came down and had a cup of tea while Mum got ready for work. When she left for work I had breakfast and then went back to bed for a bit. None of us are sleeping properly at the moment due to Dad coughing all the time.

In the late morning I decided it was play time. We all had a good play and then had another snooze on our blankets. Mum came home and had lots of bags with her, she had been hunting and got lots of food. I wanted some but Mum and Dad put it all away. After tea, we all played for a bit and then Mum fell asleep on the sofa, we all decided to join her. Dad's cough was a little bit better tonight so I think that's why Mum fell asleep.

When Mum woke up she was talking to Dad and saying that I am getting to look quite scruffy at the moment and I seem to be sprouting white hairs all over my shiny back. I like being shiny and hope I stay that way, but Mum seems to be wishing for me to be a scruffy dog. I guess we will have to wait and see what happens.

I was so tired tonight that I took myself off for a wee and then went and curled up in my crate with Teddy and hoped I would get a good night's sleep.

Friday 19th October

So this morning I got up with Mum and got on the sofa, I am really tired, Dad was coughing a lot again over night. I even wondered if there was such a thing as doggy ear defenders.

So it was pretty much a run of the mill day today. Lots to eat, lots of play and a little walk.

In the evening when Mum got home we played a lot. Mum is trying to teach me not to jump up as when she gets home I get so excited and when I jump up I am nearly as tall as her now. Apparently visitors don't like being greeted by a jumping dog. Well if they are coming to see me then of course I am bound to be happy and want to say hello.

We all ended up chilling out in the front room until it was time for bed, I went for a wee and cuddled up in my crate with Teddy and hoped I would get a full night's sleep.

Saturday 20th October

Hooray!! I got a whole night's sleep. Dad went up to bed last night and didn't get up today until late. Mum got up and made me my breakfast. After breakfast she got the scales out again. It is funny as she weighs herself first and then picks me up and weighs the both of us. She said she wont be able to do it much longer as I am getting heavy. It's quite good though because she weighs me in the kitchen and I always take the chance to have a proper look over the kitchen worktops and check there is anything I may be able to help myself to. I weighed in at 18.4kg this morning.

Mum also said that I am starting to look very scruffy, My back is now getting longer hair on it too.

We all went out in the garden for the day, Mum washed our blankets and as soon as they were dry she put them on the decking so we could all sunbathe.

Mum was taking down lots of plants, including the runner bean plant. This upset me a bit as I like picking and eating the beans, they are so tasty.

Later on in the evening we all sat and watched tv and dozed on the nice and fresh smelling blankets until it was time for bed. I had my night time wee and went into my crate with Teddy, I was still pretty tired.

Sunday 21st October

I got up this morning when Mum came and let me out of my crate. I went out for my morning wee and decided it was too cold to stay out for too long. Mum gave me my breakfast and then after a while Dad came down too.

They were looking at my feet a lot today and comparing them to a dog they had a long time ago. He was called Tramp and I know that he was very special to Mum. When they lost Zak they said they would wait a year to get another boy dog, but 2 days later there was a photo of me on facebook and they rang up about me as I looked just like Tramp did as a puppy. Well you know the rest of that story!

We had a lovely big roast dinner today, no walk today as Sunday is our lazy day. We played lots today though, Maizie is back to normal and is enjoying playing with me again. I am more careful playing with her though because she is very rough when she tells me off.

After tea, Mum had a bath so we all went in the bathroom with her and played with the bubbles in the water. It's great fun really, Rosie never seems very keen though.

Later on we all sat down and watched tv, it was really interesting, there were lots of animals on it so I watched it for ages before falling asleep on the sofa. Later on Dad woke me up and told me it was time for bed. I went out and had a night time wee and then snuggled up in my crate with Teddy.

Monday 22nd October

I got up this morning and went out in the dark for a wee. I then came back in and decided to snuggle up with Rosie and Mum on the sofa. Dad coughed a lot through the night again so we are still very tired. After Mum went to work, Dad gave us breakfast and then did the housework. We went and played outside as I couldn't be bothered to try and kill the hoover today.

Mum came home early and I was so excited again. I still got told I am not allowed to jump up but hey, you can't blame a puppy for trying. I decided that instead I would go and see what chaos I could cause in the garden. I managed to sneak behind the pond again, I thought it would be brilliant to dig a nice big hole. Mum came out and saw me. I didn't know which way to turn, I didn't want to fall in the pond again so I managed to leap over it.

Mum made me come back in doors but a few minutes later I managed to sneak out again and continue my hole digging. All was good until I got bored of that, I went to jump over the pond again and ended up losing my footing. I quietly went back in the house and Mum looked shocked. There was mud all over the kitchen floor, it was from my feet. I really didn't realise that I had made such a mess.

Mum cleaned up the mess on the floor and then I decided it was time to practice my zoomies. I am getting so fast with them now, everyone seems to look scared and moves out of the way.

By the time the evening came I was really tired so I snuggled on the blanket until bed time and then I went and cuddled up with Teddy in my crate.

Tuesday 23rd October

I woke up this morning and went out for my morning wee and then came back in and went to sleep on the sofa while Mum got ready for work. We are all still pretty tired as Dad is still coughing a lot. After Mum went to work, Dad gave us breakfast and I went out in the garden. I managed to get in behind the pond again today so I continued working on the big hole I had started to dig. Dad came out and told me off. He tried to block off the way I was getting in, but then later on I wanted to continue with my hole digging so worked out the best way to get to it was just to jump over the pond. Dad saw me do this and was really shocked. He said he was going to have to fence it off properly so I can't keep going over there. I don't see what the problem is really, I am not doing any harm to anyone.

When Mum came home she wasn't very impressed with my gardening skills. She said we used to have a nice garden, but understood that puppies like to wreck gardens until they grow up.

We lazed around in the evening and Mum played with me. She said I seem to be growing by the day. Mum was telling Dad that the vet rang today to see if I wanted to join a puppy class so I wouldn't be scared of Larrisa. I love Larrisa and am not scared of her at all so Mum said we didn't really need to go.

At the end of the evening, I was pretty tired so I took myself off to my bed and cuddled up with Teddy.

Wednesday 24th October

I got up this morning and went out in the dark to have a quick wee before coming back in and snuggling up on the sofa with Mum until she went to work. Dad got up and gave me my breakfast and then I went out to play. I also noticed that Granny and Yoyo had returned from their holidays, so I said hello to them both. I was excited to see them as it felt like it had been a long time.

I decided to find something fun to do in the garden again so I managed to jump over the pond again to return to my hole digging. Dad came and told me off and fenced off the areas he could see I was using to get to the pond. I then went off to find something else to do, I found mobiles hanging in the apple tree, they were very high up so I thought I would jump and see how high I could get. I was very surprised that I can jump up so high. I tried to get a wooden mobile, as I jumped up I could manage to grab it but I couldn't pull it off the tree. Yet again Dad told me off.

Dad ended up banning me from being unattended out in the garden after that so I went in, had lunch and had a snooze. When Mum came home we all went out into the garden and played, Mum stayed out with me and we ran up and down the garden chasing each other until we got really tired.

We came back in and I wondered if thee cat fancied a play, this then wound up the other two dogs too. Mum told me off and waved a bamboo stick at me. I ran into my crate and hid there. After a minute the cat came and sat in front of my crate almost like she was poking her tongue out at me. Mum was laughing. I started to cry because I wanted to get out of my crate, Mum then came and showed me that all I needed to have done was push the door open with my nose. I felt very silly.

In the evening we had a bit of a play, but I have settled into the routine of crashing out in the evenings now. I snoozed for ages, then had my supper and went to bed in my crate, but tonight Dad forgot to put Teddy in with me so I really hope he is ok on his own tonight.

Thursday 25th October

I woke up this morning, went for my wee and then snuggled up on the sofa with Mum. I learnt something very interesting this morning. I learnt that if you are being stroked, once the stroking stops and you don't want it to, then all you have to do is hit the person stroking you or nudge them with your nose and they will start to stroke you again. That is so brilliant and what I did all the time Mum was having her coffee.

After Mum went to work, Dad gave me my breakfast and then did the housework. It was time to try and kill that darn hoover again. I don't understand why he has to get it out every day, it gets on my nerves. After the hoover had gone we went out in the garden, Dad came out too, he says I get into too much trouble if I am out there on my own. It's not causing trouble, it's called finding fun things to do.

Later on Mum came home. I was excited as usual. She got her computer out and made a phone call, it was something to do with her work. I decided I didn't want to be ignored so I kept jumping up at her while she was on the phone. I heard her say that she was sorry but was being attacked by a playful puppy, the person on the end of the phone must have said something along the lines of "how lovely" to which Mum replied, it's a very big 18 kilo puppy and laughed

After she finished on the phone, I decided to practice my zoomies again. I am getting very good at this. But I get tired very quickly.

In the evening we all snuggled down in front of the tv. Dad stayed up later than usual and I just wanted to go to bed. I hinted a lot by yawning loudly but that didn't work so I just gave up and went to bed. I heard the tv go off after a while so I ran outside and did a quick wee and then went straight back to bed. Once again, I forgot to remind Mum and Dad to give me Teddy, but it was ok, I just went straight to sleep.

Friday 26th October

I woke up this morning, popped out for a quick wee and then went and snuggled in behind Mum on the sofa. I got Mum to stroke me loads before she went to work so that was really good.

After Mum had left, Dad gave me my breakfast and then as per usual he started to do the housework. We all went out and played in the garden for most of the day today. We think that soon the weather is going to get even colder and we may be indoors a bit more than usual. I really don't understand what is going as from when I was born it was always nice and warm. I hope that at some time it gets warm again as it is better being able to go outside and sun bathe.

Mum came home and we played a bit more, she keeps telling me I am getting to be a big boy. I enjoyed playing with Maizie and Rosie, I have to keep running between the two of them so that they both get to have a proper play with me.

Later in the evening I sneaked out and managed to wreck a few plant pots, nobody noticed so that was good. I dozed on the sofa until it was time for bed and then went into my crate and snuggled up in my crate.

Saturday 27th October

I woke up this morning and really didn't feel so good. I went out into the garden and did a massive big runny pooh. Oh my belly hurt. Dad tried giving me breakfast but I didn't want it at all.

Mum went out in the garden and saw that I had wrecked 2 plant pots, one had gladioli plants and one was rhubarb. She came in and told Dad. At this point I felt even worse. I couldn't even keep my head still as it was wobbling from side to side. Mum was really quite scared and said that she needed to ring the vet.

Mum rang the vet, she asked what I had been doing, when Mum told her and then told her my name, the vet said hello as she knew who I was right away. I have been to the vet before after eating a nail file a few weeks ago.

Anyway, the vet said I had to drink lots and eat my special anti pooh paste and that if I started to be sick I would have to go and stay at the vet. I had a massive drink of milky water and then decided I would sleep all day. I was so poorly. I didn't know eating plants could do this to me.

I popped out for a wee and saw Mum taking lots of plants from the garden and giving them to Granny to put in her garden. She said she had to do this to keep me safe.

Later on when I had woken up properly I started to feel a bit better. I didn't really want to eat much but I started to play again. Jamie and Parsla turned up in the evening so I got lots of attention, they are shocked at how big I am now. Jamie had a play with me on the floor and Parsla gave me lots of cuddles. They stayed really late, so I went and slept on the sofa until after they had gone.

Once everyone had gone home I went to bed and fell asleep right away. What a day.

Sunday 28th October

I woke up feeling quite a lot better today, but I was tired from our very late night. We usually snuggle on the sofa on a Sunday but this morning they started tidying up right away. After a while there was a knock at the door. Emma had come to see me. I really like her, she is very pretty, has very tasty hair and also she has lots of fluffy stuff on her coat and a big key ring on her handbag to die for. She gave me loads of hugs and was really shocked to see how big I was getting.

After Emma left, Dad started to cook the roast dinner and things went back to being a normal Sunday. They had their lunch and then gave us ours, I had a fab chicken dinner, I was so hungry after being poorly that I ate it really fast.

I was feeling so much better. I was sad that my lunch wasn't bigger so I kept surfing the counter to see if there was anything left on the worktop for me to eat. Mum said that we would have to clear all the worktops as I can reach everything now I am getting so tall.

In the evening it was freezing outside so we all decided to play on the blankets in the front room and then eventually we all fell asleep on the sofa, we did leave Mum a tiny bit of sofa to sit on.

Mum and Dad decided to go to bed early tonight, I was happy with that after the last few days, so I went for a wee and then went into my crate. Teddy doesn't sleep with me anymore as I have bitten him quite a lot so he has been moved upstairs to be friends with other toys that kept the dogs company when they were puppies. Mum said it is so we always have something of mine that is very special to keep. I didn't really understand that as they have me.

Monday 29th October

I woke up this morning and went out for a wee, it was very odd outside as the floor was very cold and slippery. Mum said it's call frost. I don't like it much; my toes were very cold. I didn't stay out for long and then I came back in and put my feet up on mum's back to warm them up. I stayed snuggled on the sofa until Mum went to work.

Dad made me breakfast and I really enjoyed it. I feel better again now which is good. I then did my usual trick of trying to attach that hoover again, I still haven't managed to kill it yet.

All the plants in the garden are now really boring too so I decided that I would grab the blue ball and play chase again, the other two ran after me for ages and it wore us all out.

In the evening we all snuggled down in the front room and Mum and Dad watched tv, I also watched it, it was great fun watching all sorts of different things. I really like singing the best. At the end of the night I was really tired so I took myself off for a wee and then went into my crate to go to sleep.

Tuesday 30th October

I woke up this morning and went out for my usual wee and then came in and got on the sofa with Mum and Rosie. When I went out everything was white and slippery. I had to be really careful walking as I didn't want to fall over. It was really cold on my feet again.

I am feeling my usual self again now so I gobbled up my breakfast really quickly this morning. It is very yummy but I still really wish I could eat the same food the other 2 dogs eat. Dad did the housework again, but I decided to go out and play rather than beat up the hoover.

84

When Mum came home she bought in this big orange thing that looked like a ball. She put it in the kitchen and went upstairs to get changed. When she came back she also had a box with really small knives. She got the orange ball and started cutting it with the small knives. It turns out that it is called a pumpkin. She spent ages doing stuff to it and then cut the top off it and started to scoop out this orange wet stuff. After she had finished, she put a candle in it and turned out the light. It was brilliant, the orange ball had a carving on it, the carving looked like me. I was so pleased I made her send a photo of it to the rescue centre I came from and to wish them a happy Halloween from me.

In the evening we all snuggled down in the front room to watch tv and to have a cuddle. Just before bed, Dad went and got a massive fluffy blanket, and he put it in my crate with my other ones. It looked so comfy that I decided to dash out and have my night time wee and go straight to bed. I knew I would sleep really well tonight.

Wednesday 31st October

I woke up this morning and didn't really want to go out for a wee. I was very comfy in my crate with my new massive, soft blanket. Eventually I went out and go tit over and done with. Everything in the garden is looking very sad now, the big plants are getting bare and the banana tree has gone black. It was pretty cold though.

After Mum went to work Dad did the housework and then went out into the garden. He was taking all the water out of the hot tub thing. The water was very cold but he was trying to keep me away from it as he said there were chemicals in the water. To be fair it did smell a bit funny, not like the water in the pond or in my drinking bowl.

It was a pretty usual day really, until Mum came home. She was earlier today. I was so excited that I couldn't stop jumping up at her and I did nip her a few times. But I got told off for that. I had a really good play with the other two and we all played tug of war together, it was great fun.

Mum was saying that my coat is starting to change a lot now, my back is quite scruffy now and my beard is still trying to grow. She said I would lose my shine soon. I'm not sure what that means but I hope she still loves me as much if I end up looking scruffy.

In the evening we all snuggled down in front of the tv and did a good bit of begging when Mum and Dad had some crisps. I took myself off to bed early tonight as I remembered I had that big cozy new blanket. I don't really miss Teddy anymore as I am really confident now, but I also know Teddy is safe upstairs with the teddies that Rosie and Maizie had when they were little so I know he isn't lonely.

Thursday 1st November

I woke up this morning and decided to stay in bed a bit longer as I was nice and snug in my big new blanket. I eventually got up, had a wee and then curled up on the sofa while Mum got ready for work. After she had left Dad gave me my breakfast and then as usual, did the housework. Later on he went out in the garden and let all the air out of the hot tub and took it down the shed. I had a good sniff around where the hot tub had been, there is now more room for me to play which is good.

In the afternoon I played outside with the other dogs and we played chase until no one could run anymore. Then we all came in for another nap.

When Mum came home I was really excited again, she told me off for jumping up at her and so then she got on the floor so I could say hello properly. We all had another really good play and I even tried to get the cat to join in, she chased me around the table for a bit, but I think that is because she doesn't really like me still. I wonder if she ever will. She seems ok with the other two dogs. Maybe one day she will get used to me.

Mum did a test think on the internet today and according to that I am now like a 5 year old human. Mum said that sounds right as at the moment I can be very naughty, and I have managed to wreck her lovely garden.

Mum and Dad also said it looks like I have grown even more as Rosie looks really small now. I wonder how big I am going to get. I have found my voice now as well and really enjoyed having a good old bark today, I don't sound so much like a puppy now.

In the evening, we had our usual cuddles on the sofa and then I went off for a wee and went to my crate to get comfy on my lovely blanket.

Friday 2nd November

I got up this morning and went out for my usual morning wee. I then came in and tried to push Mum forward on the sofa so I could snuggle up behind her. Mum kept telling me I was too big to squeeze in behind her but I still managed it.

After Mum went to work, Dad gave me my breakfast and then it was the normal routine for the rest of the day, walk, play, kill hoover and doze. Mum came home after work and I jumped up at her and nearly took her out. She told me off because I also get so excited that I started to nip her, apparently this is not socially acceptable for a puppy of my age.

In the evening we had a food delivery, it was Chinese and we got a few chips out of it. I then snuggled up on the sofa and decided to act a fool to make Dad laugh. I licked the sofa arm and my tongue got slower and slower and with that Dad laughed more and more. At least I have now found a way to get myself out of trouble really quickly now.

I ended up going to bed quite early this evening, I was tired and decided to go and get cozy in my big blanket.

Saturday 3rd November

I woke up later today, it wasn't very nice weather today so I quickly went out for a wee and then came back in and slept on the sofa. Mum did my breakfast today because Dad was having a lay in. When he did get up I had a big cuddle and then there was a knock at the door. It was my Aunty Bean. She had treats in her pockets, we could smell them as soon as she walked in. We decided we just needed to mug her and get all the treats, so the three of us jumped all over her and then when she sat down I got on her lap so she couldn't move and then Rosie went through her coat pockets.

We got the treats and then settled down on the blankets while the humans all sat chatting and drinking tea. Aunty Bean didn't stay too long so after she left I decided to see what was in my toy bucket today.

At the bottom of the bucket I found this thing, it was called an antler. I decided too give it a try, I loved it. I chewed it for most of the afternoon and at one point I was so engrossed in the antler that I forgot I needed a wee and I wet myself. Dad told me off but then understood it was because I was concentrating so hard on my chew.

In the evening I still kept hold of my antler. Mum thought it was funny as it had been in the toy bucket for about 5 years. Well, it's mine now so I am quite happy with that.

I stayed up a bit later tonight but then I went to sleep right away as I missed out on sleeping through the evening as I was so busy with my antler. I took myself out and had a quick wee and then went to bed.

Sunday 4th November

I woke up this morning and it was raining. I went out for a wee and when I came back in and had a shake, all my coat went really fluffy. Mum said I looked very messy.

I had breakfast and then found my antler again, I chewed it for ages and then Dad went out and came back with a stuffed bone. Well, I hid my antler away and started the chew the bone. It was very yummy. Dad then went into the kitchen and started to cook that usual big Sunday dinner. I must admit to really liking Sundays.

After lunch I went out to the loo and it was raining, I came running back in and slipped all over the kitchen floor. Once I had got into the dining room and was on the carpet, I could run faster, so I came bombing into the front room, everyone dived out of my way, it's great that they all get out of the way. I am getting really good at doing the equivalent of a hand brake turn now and can skid to a sitting halt by Mum's feet. Everyone really laughs when I do that.

In the evening I found my antler again so I amused myself with that before I went to bed. Over the last few days it has been really noisy outside in the dark with lots of banging noises. Mum and Dad just seem to ignore it so it doesn't scare me at all. I have seen some really pretty lights in the sky too. Mum said there will be lots of them tomorrow night. I will be a brave boy and not get scared.

I went off to bed tonight without any prompting. I had a wee and then settled down in my crate for the rest of the night.

Monday 5th November

I got up this morning and had my usual wee, I then went and stole Mum's place on the sofa and she had to balance on the edge. I did the nose shove thing to make her stroke me lots and then did my usual inspection of her boots when she got them out to put on. I like to shove my nose right in the boots to check there is nothing in there that shouldn't be.

When Mum had gone to work, Dad did his usual routine, this time though he took lots of rubbish out and put it in a green bag in the garden. Well, it was just the right height for me to help myself so I had a good rummage through to see if there was anything tasty in there. Dad didn't even notice what I had done.

Mum came home and noticed right away that I was out going through the rubbish so she made me come in. She then shut the dog flap. Mum also turned the tv up really loud for some reason. As it got dark, there were loads and loads of bangs and Maizie looked scared. Dad wrapped her up in a blanket so then I decided that she needed a big hug. I lay with her and put my paw on her to reassure her that everything was ok. After a while Maizie relaxed and went to sleep.

We all slept for the rest of the evening and we all ignored the noise outside. Mum and Dad were very pleased that none of us were scared. When we decided to go to bed all the noise had stopped so it was safe for us to go out and have a wee. We then all came in and went to our beds.

Tuesday 6th November

I got up this morning and went out for my wee. It was raining so I was as quick as possible. I came in and got in behind Mum on the sofa. I nudged her loads and she stroked and cuddled me until she got ready for work. When she went to the cupboard under the stairs I got excited, she was getting her boots out. I love sticking my head inside the boots in case there is something in there. There never is and Mum finds it all really funny.

Today was a typical day again, walk, play and sleep. Oh yes, and of course, attacking the hoover. Mum came home at her usual time, we had a good play and I barked, she said I sound like a big boy now as my bark is pretty low. I still don't bark at the door though, I only bark to get attention from Maizie and Rosie.

The cat was in a weird mood today, she decided to play with me a bit, so she ran around the house and ended up chasing me around the dining room table. I am really scared of her still but hopefully she will carry on making an effort with me.

In the evening, we all chilled out in front of the tv. I got up on Dad's lap for a cuddle and then at bedtime I very quickly popped out as it was raining very hard. I was quite glad to go and stretch out in my bed.

Wednesday 7th November

It was another miserable morning weather wise today. I popped out to the loo very quickly. I came back in and realised that things were different this morning. Mum hadn't gone too work today. I had breakfast and then had a bit of a play. After a while Mum and Dad started to get ready to go out. We all got into our beds and were given a treat each. Mum and Dad went out.

Mum and Dad were out for a long time today so I decided to take this opportunity to sleep. I do like my crate, I have blankets and toys to keep me amused but for me, sleep is good.

After a few hours Mum and Dad returned, they had lots of my food with them and they kept telling me what a good boy I am for being good while they were out. I was very excited to see them again as I don't usually get left for that long.

I love the way everyone takes it in turn to play with me. I feel very special.

I was quite tired in the evening and I think Rosie was too, we decided to go to bed early and we both went and got into our crates. It didn't take long for me to fall asleep today.

Thursday 8th November

I woke up really early this morning thanks to Mum. She got up at 5.30am, that's like the middle of the night I think. I couldn't even be bothered to get out of bed for a while. I then popped out for my morning wee and then went and lay behind Mum on the sofa. It was a pretty rubbish day weather wise, it was very windy and raining quite hard. I really miss those lovely sunny days from when I was little. I hope it comes back again one day as I like lying out in the sun and playing outside without getting my feet wet.

After Mum went to work, Dad did his daily battle with the hoover, I am getting really brave now and am really going to kill that thing one day. I don't like the noise it makes at all. Mum came home at the usual time and I was so excited. Just before she came home there was a knock at the door and a man delivered a big packet. Inside the packet was three antlers, they were for us. We were very happy with our antlers and played with them for ages.

After tea I decided it was time to do my zoomie training. I ran from the bottom of the garden, squeezed through the dog flap and ran so fast through the house that Rosie managed to jump sideways up on to the sofa to get out of my way. Today was the fastest zoomies I have done. At one point Mum even had to lift the cat out of my way. I was really crazy, it was great.

I got so tired from all that running that I just collapsed on the floor panting and then eventually fell asleep. I only ended up waking up so I could have a quick wee and go off to my crate to get some proper sleep.

Friday 9th November

91

I woke up early again this morning. I don't understand why Mum gets up so early. I stayed in bed for a bit and then eventually got up and went out for a wee. It was pretty cold and gloomy outside so I came back in and went onto the sofa to sleep. Mum got ready for work and I inspected her boots like I do every morning.

After Mum went to work, Dad did the usual chores and we had the usual day, walk, play eat. I do quite like my life. Later on, Mum came back home. I was really excited and jumped all over her. She told me not to jump up but I really can't help it. I suppose when I get older I will be able to curb my excitement a bit.

After tea, I thought I would practice my zoomies again. Everyone gets out of my way really quickly now as they can hear me coming. I am getting so fast now. Apparently Dad said I am ruining the carpet with my claws from where I skid to a halt. I think the carpet looks ok still. After my run about I settled down on the blanket for the night until bed time and then I went into my crate to go to sleep.

Saturday 10th November

I had a lay in this morning. Mum didn't get up til around 8am which I know now means she isn't going to work. I was very pleased about this. The weather is still bad but at least it was only raining on and off today. Mum gave me breakfast and then Mum weighed me again. This week I weighed in at 19.9kg. Mum said I am getting too heavy to lift up now, but she did manage it.

I helped Mum a lot today, I helped her with the housework and then I went out into the garden with her and we looked around and did a bit of clearing leaves. Mum noticed that I had been fooling around by the pond again as the netting was broken on the pond and the wooden bar across the middle had half fallen in the water. I didn't have the heart to tell Mum I had fallen in the water again.

I played with the other dogs for ages and got them both to chase me until they were very tired. It was good fun and I can run for much longer than the other two.

In the evening I got on my blanket and pretty much slept all evening, so did Maizie and Rosie. We only bothered to wake up to get some snacks when Mum and Dad made some food. I have now totally mastered the art of begging, I just tilt my head to the side and stare intently and this seems to really work.

I didn't stay up too late tonight so I decided to go and have my final wee of the night and then took myself off to bed and snuggled up with my blanket.

Sunday 11th November

I woke up late again this morning as Mum had a lay in. I took myself off out for a wee and then when I got back in the tv was on and there were lots of people on it. It was very weird because I felt like something was wrong with my eyes, one minute the tv had lots of colour like it usually does and then suddenly all the colour would go. Me and Rosie enjoyed watching it though and at 11am Mum and dad went all quiet for a little bit. Apparently 100 years ago there was a lot of fighting which stopped on this day. Mum said that even dogs and horses went to fight too and many died. That made me sad.

Mum also said that they used to use greyhounds in the war for a short time but had to change to lurchers as greyhounds would get bored after running for a bit and get distracted and not pass on the messages they were meant to, so they used lurchers instead as they were better. Charming.

Dad went out and cooked the Sunday roast again today, and after we all got ours. I noticed that this week I had a few extra bits in my dinner, I also had potato and carrots. It was yummy.

After lunch we were all full and tired so we slept on the blankets until early evening and then I decided it was playtime again. I did zoomies around the house and garden and went searching for toys to play with that were outside. I came back with this spikey thing. Mum said it was a bit from the pond filter and took it off me and said she would put it back in when she cleaned it again.

I eventually tired myself out and decided to have an early night and go and cuddle up in my blankets in the crate.

Monday 12th November

I woke up this morning early because it is a Mum goes to work day. I stayed in my crate for a little bit but then I needed a wee so I braved the thundery weather and popped out. I came back in and then cuddled up with Mum. I wanted to play with her but I got told off for being a bit rough as I am enjoying having these new massive teeth.

Dad did his usual housework and then went out for a bit in the late afternoon. Mum came home and I was really excited. She decided to take us for a walk right away. I don't think she will do that again because I was still so excited that she was home that I bounced up the road. It took me ages to calm down and walk properly. She kept getting all our leads tangled up too which I found amusing. Mum was doing something called power walking, I thought she was just rushing, I wanted to check all the drive ways that we passed but there was no time for that.

When we got home we were all really hot and tired so we all got on the sofa and had a snooze. We soon woke up when Dad came back as we were hungry and wanted our tea.

In the evening I had a really good play with Mum. I lay on her lap and we pulled silly faces at her phone and we got lots of silly photographs. It was very good fun. After that I went out for a quick wee and then went to bed. I was very tired this evening.

Tuesday 13th November

I got up this morning and went for my usual wee and cuddled up on the sofa. I decided this morning that I needed more room and worked out that if I put my paws behind Mum's back then I could push her towards the edge of the sofa and give myself a lot more room. Mum went to work and Dad popped out on his bike, it was really weird as he came home quite quickly but he was driving Mum's car. So where was Mum? I was confused and concerned.

Dad did all the housework and I chased the hoover again. I still haven't managed to kill it yet. Maybe one day. It is just the most annoying thing.

Mum came home a bit earlier today as she had some work to do from home, she said she needed to be home half an hour before her telephone meeting or I would still be hyper and annoy Mum when she was on the phone.

After the phone meeting Mum played with me and the other two dogs. We played ball and also pully. We played until we couldn't play anymore. We then all crashed out in front of the tv and dozed until bedtime, I then took myself off for a wee and went to my crate to sleep.

Wednesday 14th November

I got up later today. Mum had a day off work. We sat snuggled up on the sofa and then there was a knock at the door. It was Parsla. I was so happy to see her, she is great, she makes us dog toys and also brings us treats. I got on her lap and kissed her loads. Mum and Dad kept telling me to get off. But Parsla didn't mind. It was wonderful to see her.

After Parsla left I went out and chased Rosie up and down the garden for ages. I got so out of breath that I came in and had a quick power nap. I woke up when I heard Mum go out the back door. She said she wanted to repair all the damage I had caused in the garden. She started off by taking all the netting off the pond. She put new netting up and then built a fence around the pond to stop me from falling in anymore. Then she got out this really noisy thing, I was just totally shocked, it was an outdoor hoover. It was massive and really noisy. I tried really hard to kill it, I bit it, I barked at it and at one point I misjudged and actually bit Mum's leg. She was not impressed. I helped her all afternoon in the garden. I do have to admit that it looked much better after she had finished and because all the leaves had gone, I could see where I was running better. Our lawn also looked really good so we decided to have a little play on it as Mum was finishing up.

In the evening we were all very tired from all we did today so we cuddled up together on the sofa and slept right up until bedtime. I really enjoyed myself today. But now I have two hoovers that I need to kill.

Thursday 15ᵗʰ November

This morning I got up just after Mum and went out to the garden. It is nice to see it looking tidy, all that is missing is the sunshine. I came back in and cuddled up on the sofa. I stayed there until Mum got her boots out and then I did a full boot inspection and checked each one for spiders and things. I don't want Mum to have any shocks.

After Mum went to work I assisted Dad with the housework again and had yet another attempt at killing the hoover. Dad kept telling me to stop but I have now worked out that I can talk back to hm and he seems to understand what I am saying. He talks to me, I smile and talk and sneeze a lot and then it makes Dad laugh. It's pretty good as I am now using this to get myself out of sticky situations like when I get told off for chasing the cat. When the cat chases me, she doesn't get told off. I think that's a bit unfair.

Mum came home and we had a good play, she went out in the garden to check that I hadn't wrecked anything. The pond netting is still intact, mainly because it is far too cold now to attempt a swim. In the evening I practiced my talking again and made both Mum and Dad laugh. Then I went and lay down on the blankets and stretched myself out as long as I could get.

I went to bed quite early tonight as I was pretty tired from an early start this morning. I went out for my wee and then cuddled up in my blankets in the crate.

Friday 16ᵗʰ November

I woke up this morning and really didn't want to get up today. I stayed in my crate for quite a while until I really needed a wee. I came back in and snuggled up with Mum until she went to work. After Mum went to work I had breakfast and then helped Dad with the housework. It was a bit rainy today so I didn't go out much and as for go for a walk, no thank you. It is getting a lot colder now so I am glad I am growing a new hairy coat. I am starting to look rather smart I think.

Mum came home and had been to the shop on her way home, there were lots of nice smells coming out of the bag. I smiled and talked to her to see if she would give me something out of the bag but she didn't. But I did get a chew.

I had a really good play and then lay down with the other two dogs on the blanket. We all snuggled up together to keep warm. We stayed there until bedtime and then I went off into my crate to get a good night's sleep.

Saturday 17th November

I woke up this morning a bit later than usual. Mum had a lay in. I didn't really mind though. After Mum had had her coffee she gave me my breakfast and then weighed me. I am now 20.1kg. Mum seems to find it hard to pick me up now and said I am getting really heavy.

After Dad got up, Mum went out into the garden and caught me being naughty. I have discovered a way to get to the little pond. The only problem is that I knocked a big plant pot into the pond and knocked a load of the edging slabs into the water. To try and save myself from a telling off, I jumped the little fence and then limped my way back up the garden. I thought I would pretend that I had hurt my back leg. Mum looked worried for a minute and then said that she had rumbled me and knew I was faking. Perhaps next time I need to do the scream of death with it. That may look more convincing.

In the afternoon I decided I wanted to play chase with the dogs so I grabbed the infamous blue ball and off we went. Mum was trying to tidy up the garden and kept standing dead still as we ran past. At least she realises that we calculate our routes very carefully and she doesn't move into our path. She held up her phone thing and videoed us running up and down. We all get very tired.

In the evening we all chilled out in the front room. Mum and Dad watched the tv and the rest of us dozed on the blankets. We woke up when it was time to beg for treats but that was about it. We then went out for our evening wee and all settled down to go to bed.

Sunday 18th November

I got fed up with waiting for Mum to get up this morning so I decided to raise the alarm by doing my not too loud bark. It worked, Mum got up. She must have thought I really needed a wee. I didn't, I was just a bit bored and was properly awake. Dad got up about an hour later and they started to watch Hollyoaks on tv. I really like the theme tune to that so every time the adverts came on I would look at the tv and tilt my head to one side. I like it when I make them laugh.

Mum went out in the care for a bit and when she came back the other two dogs got all excited. Mum had these green woollen things. Maizie and Rosie lined up and sat patiently waiting for the woollen things. They were jumpers. Rosie had hers put on first and then I decided to butt in and get mine on. Lastly Maizie had hers put on. We all matched. They are called Christmas jumpers. Dad said it was too early for us to wear them but Mum said she wanted to check the sizes of them.

We stayed in our jumpers all day and it was great when we went out. I didn't feel the cold at all. We had a lovely roast dinner again and I am noticing that every week there is more and more different things in my dish. This time I had a bit of roast potato.

Mum and Dad watched tv in the evening and I got a bit hot in my jumper so Mum helped me to take it off. Just before bed she took Rosie's off as well but Rosie wasn't happy about it and was growling as Mum took it off. She told her she could have it back tomorrow. Maizie just hid in her bed and that seemed to work as Mum didn't take her jumper off. Mum did say that me and Rosie have blankets in our beds but Maizie doesn't so perhaps that's why she kept hers on.

We went to bed quite early tonight, but it had been a very tiring weekend. We all went out for our late night wee and then all went to our beds to go to sleep. I think Maizie was probably the cosiest dog out of us all.

Monday 19th November

I woke up this morning and went out for a wee, it was really freezing. Maizie was still wearing her Christmas jumper so she wasn't as cold as me. I came back in and cuddled up with Mum on the sofa while she had her coffee. I didn't try and push Mum off the sofa this morning as it was nice to cuddle into her as she was so warm.

After Mum went to work I helped Dad with the housework and then tried yet again to kill the hoover. I then went out and caused more mayhem in the garden. Dad came out and had to re fence the little pond as I had been in it yet again. Mum came home and had a massive black sack, I was excited to see what was in it. How boring, it was bubble wrap. Mum took it out to the garden so I went out to see what she was going to do with it. It was very strange because she started to wrap it around the banana trees. Perhaps they were cold too.

In the evening we all cuddled up on the sofa. I cuddled into Mum and then suddenly Rosie ran across me and got on Mum's lap. She started to smile at me, I think she wanted Mum all to herself. I didn't budge though and stood my ground. If I want cuddles with Mum I shall jolly well do so.

Mum and Dad seemed very tired so we all went to bed pretty early tonight. I went out in the cold for my bedtime wee and then sank into my blankets and went to sleep.

Tuesday 20th November

I woke up this morning and stayed in my crate for a bit as it was really cold again. Eventually I got up and had a wee and then curled up in a ball next to Mum while she had her morning coffee.

Dad then got up so we all got up like we usually do to greet him. Me and Maizie always follow Dad into the loo first thing and we always sniff his wee. We feel we have to do this as we know Dad isn't very well and we can keep a check on him and alert Mum if it all gets really weird.

I helped Dad with he housework and then went out and yet again I trashed the garden. I like the little pond at the bottom of the garden and even though Dad fences it off I can still get in there. I knocked that plant pot into the pond again. Mum came home and saw what I had done and tutted at me. I followed her back in doors with my tail between my legs. I am getting good at making Mum feel sorry for me when I have been naughty.

In the evening we all crashed out on the blankets and stayed there until it was time for bed. Maizie went to bed yet again with her Christmas jumper on. I didn't need mine as my crate is nice and warm.

Wednesday 21st November

Today I got up late, Mum had the day off work, Yippeeee!! I went out for my wee and then snuggled up with Mum and stayed there for ages as she didn't have to get ready so early. When she had woken up a bit we played with my toys. Mum said I seem to be growing every day at the minute. I am 24 inches tall to my shoulder at the moment and Mum says I still have some growing to do.

I have now completely sussed out begging and also nudging to get attention. Its great, I put my paw on Mum and she strokes me. I wish I had learnt this earlier. Begging is brilliant, you sit and stare as hard as you can at the person eating and the minute they look at you, you sort of lean forward just a little bit and they seem to give in and you get some food. It's all pretty clever stuff.

Mum and Dad went out in the afternoon so I went into my crate and slept. I had my antler in with me but I couldn't be bothered to chew it, so I thought I would get some sleep so I could play more once Mu and Dad got back.

When they returned they gave me my dinner and then I played with Rosie and Maizie, they still like to take it in turns to play with me so I don't get overwhelmed.

In the evening we all got up on the sofa with Mum and watched some tv with her until it was time to go to bed.

Thursday 22ⁿᵈ November

I got up this morning and it was really cold again. I was glad though that the decking outside wasn't slippery today. I had a quick wee and then went back in to cuddle up with Mum. I really think Mum is going to have to get a bigger sofa soon as I already take up two seats, Rosie manages to squeeze in still or sits on top of me.

After Mum went to work, Dad did the housework and I went out to play in the little pond again. Dad told me off so I came back in. I did manage to get back to the pond a few more times but every time I got caught down there Dad would tell me off. In the end I decided to play with the other dogs instead.

When Mum came home Dad told her that I had been very naughty today so I decided that I would be really good for the rest of the day. I greeted her when she came in. I am getting so tall now that when I jump up I can nearly reach her face. I love the fact I am getting bigger. I can see so much more now, I can even reach anything that is left on the kitchen worktop.

The rest of the day was pretty usual really, then Mum said she was going to bed. I went out for my night time wee but got distracted with the little pond again, Dad shouted for me to come back in. I had found a little glass candle holder and had bought it back in with me. Dad asked me what it was and I thought to myself "Oh oh", so I quickly dropped it on the kitchen floor. It broke into lots of bits. I quickly ran to my crate and Dad shut the door. I didn't even get my bed time biscuit tonight. Tomorrow I shall try harder to be good.

Friday 23ʳᵈ November

I woke up this morning and went and lay on Mum's lap. I have mastered getting her to stroke me now. Nose nudging is really good. Mum went to work and used Dad's car today so he was home with us all day. I was a bit of a pain today Dad said. I have found new ways to get into the bushes in the garden so Dad was trying to block it off.

Mum came home from work and I was so excited that I bit her on the bum. I have noticed that when I get told off Mum and Dad point at me when they say no. I really don't like this so I smile and show my teeth and bark back at them. I think this is good fun. I can't help being excited though and it makes me want to bite. Apparently I will grow out of this a some point.

After tea, Jamie came over, I was really excited to see him too and jumped all over him. It took me ages to calm down. I love having visitors, it's great fun. Jamie stayed for ages and then later in the evening his girlfriend Parsla came to take him home. We had a very late night and I was really glad to get to bed tonight.

Saturday 24th November

I really didn't want to get up today, I was really tired as I didn't get to bed until around 2am. I managed to go out for a wee and then I went back to sleep on the sofa. I got weighed again today so today I was 20.3kg. Dad was a bit concerned that I hadn't put much weight on this week, but I think next week I will be heavier.

Mum popped out in her car this morning and when she came home I was really pleased because she had Jamie with her. It was brilliant to see him again. He didn't stay very long today so after he went I went out in the garden with the other dogs and we chased each other around until we were all really tired out.

We didn't do much really apart from play as Dad wasn't too well today again. I feel sorry for him so I make sure I give him loads of cuddles to try and make him feel better. In the evening we all curled up on the sofa and watched tv. Mum went to bed pretty early tonight and I also went into my crate until Dad told us it was bedtime. I then went for my evening wee and went back into my crate to get a good night's sleep.

Sunday 25th November

I woke up this morning and remembered it is naughty day. Mum and Dad say that every Sunday I get naughty. I had a long zoomie session in the garden and then came back in as Mum had this noisy machine outside that sprayed water everywhere. Apparently the decking is getting slippery and Mum was worried that I may hurt myself so she went out and washed it all down. Then after she finished she tidied up the garden a bit and then came in the house and was soaking wet and looked really cold. She went in the bathroom and got changed and then came in the front room and sat on the sofa.

I sat on her lap and her legs were freezing. I didn't sit there for long, but I wanted to go and see what she had been doing anyway. I went out in the garden and it was great, she had stopped all the decking from being slippery. I had to test this out so I ran up and down and all was good.

In the afternoon we had our roast dinner, every week I get new things in my roast. This week I had cauliflower added. That was really yummy. After lunch Mum and Dad watched Hollyoaks, I really like the music for that and every time the adverts came on I would look at the tv and Mum and Dad would laugh.

In the evening we all got cozy on the sofa and stayed there until it was time for bed.

Monday 26th November

I got up this morning and went out for my morning wee and then came back in and got on the sofa. I had a really nice cuddle with Mum while she drank her coffee and then proceeded to try and push her off with my feet. I like to stretch and push as it looks like I am not doing it on purpose.

Mum went off to work and Dad did the housework, I tried yet again to kill the hoover. I didn't succeed but then I am getting used to that. For my next mission I decided to try and get the cat to play with me. She does give in and chase me on occasion but on the whole I think she just wants to be left alone. Maizie was in a really playful mood today so we played a lot. I think Rosie was glad of the rest to be fair.

When Mum came home she let us all out in the garden, the dog flap was opened. We played outside for ages, and then decided to come back in. Rosie stayed out in the garden. Mum thought it was very odd as she could see that the bushes were moving by Rosie. As she got closer she could see Rosie had got herself in a bit of a pickle. We had been climbing through the bushes to check Maizie hadn't buried anything and Rosie had got tangled up in the solar light cables. Mum shouted at her to stay still and went up to her and untangled her. Yay, Rosie was free at last.

After all that we decided that we would stay indoors, it was getting cold so we stayed in and continued to play for ages. Mum played the pointing game with me which made me bark, she said she is going to teach me to attack on command so she feels safe when we are all out on our own with Mum. She doesn't need to teach me as I would always look after my family.

We cozied up in the evening on our blankets until it was time for bed.

Tuesday 27th November

I got up this morning and went for my usual wee before going and getting up on the sofa with Mum. It was raining again. It always seems to be raining now. I really don't like it. I hate the way it makes my coat stick out everywhere and I just generally don't like getting wet unless it is because I am playing with a hose, or a pond.

I assisted Dad with the housework like I usually do and still haven't managed to kill the hoover. I will keep trying and one day I will get it. I went and found a woolly ball and convinced the other two dogs to play with me. We played again for ages. Once again it was a usual day, eat, sleep , walk around the block and sleep again.

Mum came home and I was jumping all over her. She is starting to get really annoyed when I nip her, this is only because I am just so excited when she gets home. We had a good play and Rosie ended up having to have some time out in her crate as she was getting way to hectic even for me. After she calmed down she came back out and we had more cuddles on the sofa.

In the evening we played a bit more and I watched a bit of tv between dozing and playing. It was a pretty nice evening really. Mum and Dad stayed up later than usual. They keep watching this thing on tv with a bald man who has a big moustache. It's called breaking bad apparently. They stayed up and watched quite a lot of it. I ended up taking myself off for a wee and went to bed on my own.

Wednesday 28th November

I stayed in bed later today. Mum had the day off work. When I did finally get up it was raining again. Mum told me that she is getting fed up with it too. We snuggled on the sofa for ages this morning, it was really lovely that Mum didn't go out first thing.

Mum went out about 11am, she said she was meeting ParIsa and going to see the Queen. Well I wanted to go too but I wasn't allowed. Mum went off so I amused myself by helping Dad out and getting my daily massage from him.

Mum came back eventually, she hadn't been to see the Queen, she had been to the cinema to see a film about a band called Queen. She started to measure up the top of my crate and said her keyboard would fit nicely on the top of it. Dad wasn't very amused and said it would be more for him to dust.

A bit later on me and Rosie decided to have a good play, it was great fun until Rosie got bored. Once that happened I decided to go outside and play on my own. When I got bored of that because it started to rain, I came back in through the dog flap and and ran as fast as I could through the house. My timing for this was all wrong, I crashed into Rosie and landed on Mum. Rosie made a loud grunt and Mum shouted ouch at the top of her voice. Rosie quickly got up on the sofa to get a cuddle off Mum and seemed better right away but Mum rubbed her own leg for ages. Mu said that I was getting so big now that I need to be more careful as I could hurt everyone now. Apparently I am very heavy and really big now compared to the other two. I will be more careful now as I really don't want to hurt anyone.

We all spent the evening in the front room together and then went to bed at a better time tonight.

Thursday 29th November

I woke up this morning and did not want to get up at all. It had been so stormy and windy in the night that it kept waking me up. When I eventually did get up I noticed that our garden swing had moved to the middle of the garden. It is really heavy and I was shocked it had moved. I came back in and cuddled up on the sofa with Mum.

After Mum went to work, Dad did the housework and then I did my usual efforts at killing the hoover. It was a usual day of playing, eating sleeping and walking and generally run of the mill until the evening. In the evening once we had all had our tea, a friend of Mum and dad's came to see us. She was lovely and really good fun. She was called Nadine and I felt safe with her as could see Mum and Dad really liked her. She played with me quite a bit and I really liked having her here. When she left I was quite sad, the house was quiet after she left.

We all fell asleep pretty much after Nadine left and then we went out for a wee and all went to bed pretty early.

Friday 30ᵗʰ November

I got up this morning and went out for a wee, I then went and snuggled on the sofa until Mum went for her morning shower. So every morning when Mum gets in the shower she feeds the cat and shuts the baby gate. Rosie is very clever and she jumps it to try and get in the bathroom. I still am not brave enough to try and jump it so I always wait for Mum to let me in.

Mum went to work and Dad did the housework and then popped out to get some shopping. He came back with with some nice treats for us. I was very happy with this.

When Mum came home I heard Dad tell her that I have trashed a bit more of the garden. Well' I hadn't, I just wanted to get into the bit of ground under the nut tree as I can smell that things have been buried there by Maizie. Dad said that when the weather is a bit better he is going to stop me getting in there once and for all.

In the evening we all crashed out in the front room and we even got some pizza, it was quite a nice evening. I ended up belly up on my blanket. I stayed like that until it was time to go to bed.

Saturday 1ˢᵗ December

I got a lay in this morning. Once Mum got up I stayed in bed a bit longer until I really needed a wee. After breakfast Mum weighed me again, I don't really like being picked up anymore as I know Mum finds it hard to pick me up now. I weighed in at 20.7kg. Mum put my weight on her facebook and then a lady who lives with my brother said that he weighs 21kg. I need to eat more I have decided.

In the afternoon we all had a really good play time and then we started to notice that Mum and Dad looked like they were getting ready to go out. We know when they are going out without us because Mum only wears jeans or trousers when she is taking us out and she had just put her skirt on.

They went out and left us listening to classical music. I have a big cover over my crate because Maizie used to pick on me and bark at me when I was a puppy. Well, she doesn't do that anymore and I really wanted to be able to see the door for when Mum and Dad got home. I managed to pull loads of the covers up so I could see out but I felt something fall over above me. It turns out I knocked a plant over.

Mum and Dad came home and saw shat I had done and said next time they will leave the covers up so I can see out better. I think that is a good plan. We all went in the front room and had cuddles until it was time to go to bed.

Sunday 2nd December

I had another lay in today and soon realised it was Sunday. I love Sundays as we have a very lazy day and we all get a nice big roast dinner. I went out for my morning wee and then went and cuddled up with Rosie on the sofa. Mum and Dad put the tv on and we watched Hollyoaks, I absolutely love the music that is played in that. Every time I hear it I stop whatever I am doing to look at the tv. Mum and Dad think this is really funny.

Once Mum and Dad had had their dinner, Mum went out in the kitchen to do ours. I got very excited and actually barked at Mum to get her to hurry up and dish up our dinner. The cat always gets hers first which I think is a bit unfair. Dinner was great, I had more new things in my dish this week and more veg that usual. It was really yummy.

After lunch we all went into the front room and watched tv. We were all very full so we all fell asleep while Mum and Dad watched films.

We were all really lazy today and did nothing at all until it was time to go to bed. I got a bit naughty and managed to steal a pizza wrapper out of the bin. I ran down the garden with it and refused to come back. Dad got a bit annoyed as I wouldn't come back in. Eventually I decided I had better do as Dad asked or I wouldn't get my evening biscuit. I came back in and gave Dad my best sorry look when I got in my crate. He was ok because he smiled at me as he said goodnight.

Monday 3rd December

This morning yet again I really didn't want to get up. Eventually I did and then went for a quick wee and snuggled on the sofa with Mum until she went to work.

It was just a typical day really and I won't bore you with the eat, sleep walk bit so I will just skip to the evening today.

Mum came home and as she walked in the door Rosie actually said hello to Mum. Apparently she used to do it all the time but stopped after Zak died. It really does sound like she can talk. I may have to learn to do that too. We all had our tea and then went into the front room. Mum started to take some photos of me and then she started doing something with the photos on her phone. It was really funny, I was singing. I sang a song about Evesham rescue centre, where I was born and she then put it on facebook. She also sent it to the rescue centre. It was really funny, but to be fair I looked very cute.

Mum also put it on a sighthound facebook page and lots of people liked it. She said it is good to get the rescue centre noticed and then hopefully more people will help them to give more lurchers and greyhound new homes. I was pleased she did this as I got my home from facebook. I also decided tonight that I am going to return my old ID badge and collar to the centre as I am going to stay here forever now and I think it would be nice for another pup to have it.

Well after the excitement of the evening, I had a shoulder massage from Dad and a cuddle with Mum and then I was ready for bed. My day as a puppy Rockstar was brilliant but then I got really tired and went to bed. Perhaps I would dream I was doing a duet with AC/DC.

Tuesday 4th December

I woke up this morning and decided to have a bit of a lay in. It was all rainy and windy and I decided to see how long I would go without having a wee. Eventually I went out and then cuddled up with Mum for a bit.

After Mum went to work Dad did the housework again and yet again I tried to kill the hoover. It was a usual day really and there was nothing really to report until Mum got home. When she got home I was really excited again, I got told off for nipping but Mum can't understand that I can't help myself. We had a good play and Mum took a video of me running around. She put it on facebook but made it appear a bit faster. She said it could do with some Benny Hill music to go with it, whatever that is.

Mum and Dad watched some tv in the evening and then we all went to bed as they said we have a lot to do tomorrow, but they also said they were worried how I was going to react. I am a bit nervous now as I don't know what is going on.

Wednesday 5th December

I had a bit of a lay in again today as Mum was off work. I eventually got up and went for my morning wee and then snuggled on the sofa. Not long after I could see something in the window, when I looked properly I could see it was Parsla. I was so excited to see her. Mum went and let her in and then I ran as fast as I could to say hello.

Mum made Parsla a cup of tea and I noticed she had a hair tie in, I love removing them so I did. Every time she got it back off me and did her hair, I climbed behind her and took it out again. Parsla then got a ball of wool out and gave it to me. I unravelled it all over the dining room and me and the cat got totally tangled up in it. Dad came down and wondered what was going on. Parsla then did some crochet and made me and Maizie a toy each while Rosie just sat and watched.

After Parsla had gone Mum and Dad went upstairs and then came down with lots of bags and boxes. Rosie was really excited. Mum started getting out all this sparkly stuff and started to hang it off the walls, then they got 2 trees, I didn't realise you could keep trees in boxes but it appears that you can.

They then put lots of lights and things on the tree and Mum put a paw print from Zak on the tree, she looked quite sad when she did that so I got up and started to mess around to try and cheer her up. I don't think she really liked putting all that stuff up as I could hear her swearing a lot.

Once all the decorations were done, Dad came down with a massive hoover, I haven't seen that one before. It was very loud and I wasn't brave enough to attack it.

In the evening we all lay down and I just spent the evening looking at the decorations. It was very pretty. I went to bed tonight thinking about why the house looks like it does now.

Thursday 6th December

I got up this morning and all the decorations were still there. I walked into the front room and decided to see what the stockings on the fireplace were for or if there was anything in them. Well, as soon as I went over, Rosie ran over to me and pushed me out of the way and growled. It would seem I am not allowed to look at the stockings.

Mum went to work and Dad did the housework and then went shopping, or as we call it, hunting. He came back with lots of nice stuff and even some treats for us.

When Mum got home she put up even more lights and I have to say that the house is looking very pretty now. They don't even need to put the big light on in the front room anymore. Mum put her computer on and started to laugh, someone had put the music onto the video of us running around.

In the evening we were all really tired from all the excitement of the decorations still and playing with our new toys that Parlsa made yesterday. We all cuddled up on the sofa until bed time.

At bedtime I went out for a wee and I could sense there was something in the garden. I had to alert the others. I did my biggest, deepest bark and then Dad came out to see what was going on. He couldn't see anything and so reassured me that everything was ok and eventually I agreed with him and came back in and went to bed.

Friday 7ᵗʰ December

I woke up this morning and went out for a morning wee in the rain again. How how I miss the sunny days of my puppyhood. I then curled up on the sofa for a while as Mum got ready for work. When Dad woke up and came down I climbed on his lap for my usual shoulder rub. I like to do this every morning. It is very nice and I know Dad enjoys it too.

Mum went off to work and Dad did the housework, I nearly killed the hoover this morning but it still seems to be alive. It's very tough. Dad then went and did some shopping and bought back a whole box of my puppy food.

The rest of the day was as per usual really, walk, sleep, play and my favorite, eat!

Mum came home and I got really excited, she is still trying to teach me not to jump up at her but it isn't working at the moment. I don't think she really minds though.

In the evening we all settled down in front of the tv, we also all got a little bit of pizza, it was very yummy. In the end when Mum went to bed I decided to go and have my last wee of the night and then went into my crate.

Saturday 8ᵗʰ December

Yay, it's the weekend. I know this now as Mum didn't get up early. I had a wee and then got up on the sofa and dozed until it was breakfast time. Dad gave me my breakfast and then it was the usual weigh in day, today I am 21.3kg and I am 26 inches tall. Mum said her friends on the computer were saying I am going to be as big as a horse. I really hope not as I wont fit in the house anymore.

Mum got some stuff and wrapped it all up in paper, she then put all the packets under the lit up tree. It's silly because now it's all wrapped up I cant see what it is. I may have to take the paper off at some point so I can see what they are again.

It was a very rainy day today so we all decided to stay in, I only popped out for toilet purposes today and spent my time playing with the dogs and with Mum and Dad.

We had quite a lazy day today and just chilled out in front of the tv for most of the evening. It was an ok day though and at least none of us got into any trouble.

Sunday 9th December

I woke up late again this morning and got up on the sofa, I know what day it is today, it's roast and twangy music day. It wasn't long before that music came on again. I love it. Apparently its called the Hollyoaks theme tune. I especially love the very end bit. Every time I hear it I run to the tv. Dad went out and cooked roast, today it was pheasant. Dad bought one home yesterday and I have to say, Mum did not seem very happy at all with this. She said there was no need. Anyway. Once they had their dinner, Mum got ours ready, she gave some to the cat and she didn't want it. So then to my pleasure I saw her empty the cat's dish into my bowl. Whoopie, I got extra today.

In the afternoon I thought I would make Mum and Dad laugh a lot so I started to mime. I have now learnt the art of quiet speech. Mum and Dad thought it was very funny. We all settled down to watch tv for the rest of the day. I love Sundays because we don't do anything at all, it is a real lazy day. We all went to bed earlier tonight because Mum has to go back to work tomorrow. We all had a wee and then went to our beds to go to sleep.

Monday 10th December

I woke up early this morning when Mum came down. I went and lay on the sofa. Mum seemed a bit stressed today. She was ironing her skirt for work and put a big hole in it. She said she thought today was going to be a bad Monday.

After she went to work I had the usual day with Dad, it was ok, I still didn't manage to kill the hoover though.

Mum came home and things got a bit weird. We all went out to play with the ball and as me and Rosie were running Maizie grabbed Rosie, well

113

what a noise, they had a fight. Mum ended up grabbing Rosie and put her in her crate to calm her down. Once Rosie seemed calmer, Mum let her out again. I couldn't believe it, she was still angry and ran over to Maizie and started to fight again. I ran away out through the dog flap. I didn't want to end up in the fight. I don't understand why they fell out.

So Rosie spent a longer time in her crate until she was calm again. Mum checked them both over and it all looked ok, it would seem that it was mainly noise they made and didn't hurt each other.

I think girls just get cross easier than boys. Luckily no harm was done and all was good for the rest of the evening. Mum seemed very sad though. She had a hard day at work and having Rosie and Maizie fighting upset her.

Mum went to bed a bit earlier today as she said she wanted today to be over. I have to say that I agreed with this so I went out for a quick wee and then went to my crate to fall asleep so tomorrow would come quicker.

Tuesday 11th December

I woke up today and eventually got out of bed. I went for a wee and then got on the sofa with Rosie. Rosie and Maizie seem to have forgotten about yesterday and I was very pleased about this. I didn't like it yesterday when they fell out. Dad gave me breakfast and then did the housework. Yet again I tried to kill the hoover. I am just going to go for it properly soon I think.

I had a good day and played with the other dogs and had an afternoon nap while I waited for Mum to get home.

Once Mum was home she went and got changed into jeans, we love it when she has her jeans on as that is her taking us out clothes. It is really hard for us to guess when we are going out with Dad as he wears the same clothes when he takes us out but Mum only wears her jeans when she is coming out with us.

I am still a little bit of a novice on the lead and I have to walk between Rosie and Maizie as that was my puppy routine, although now I am so big I am the protector instead of being protected. It was nice going out in the dark because the streets all have lots of lights like in our house. I'm only used to lots of lights outside in the summer like the ones in our garden when I was a pup.

When we got home we all had a big drink, some tea and then curled up on our blankets. The other dogs eventually got on the sofa so I had the blankets all to myself. I decided to re arrange the blankets but got so carried away that I actually did a wee on it. I was so ashamed. I don't have a clue why I even did it. Mu took the blankets and washed them. I went to bed because I didn't want to lay on the floor and the sofa was full of girl dogs.

Wednesday 12th December

I got up this morning, went for my wee and then noticed there were nice clean and dry blankets on the floor so I went and lay on them. They smelt lovely. Perhaps next time they start smelling doggy I will have another accident. Mum went off to work and Dad gave me my breakfast.

It was another usual day with not a lot to report until Mum got home. I was not impressed. All I could smell was loads of other dogs. Mum said there were 10 dogs she had been stroking. She had been to Lisa's to collect a painting for a friend, Lisa is the one who painted Zak for Mum after he passed away. This picture was really lovely, but the dog looked strange as he was short and fat, not like me. I could have out run him easily.

Anyway, eventually I let her off and spent the evening having lots of cuddles. Mum told Dad today that I actually look like a grown up dog quite a bit now. I am indeed a very big boy now. Mum and Dad said it really doesn't matter how big I get now as they love me and would never let me go back to the rescue centre. I went to bed very happy tonight. I am definitely here forever now.

Thursday 13th December

I got up this morning and.....stuff the usual talk, today was epic. After all these months of learning about the cat, I now know why the other dogs don't worry about her. So the cat, the thing with knives on her hands, who tries to get me all the time when I say hi, does indeed have a good point! Today at tea time we were all fed. Well you know me, no dinner could ever be big enough for me. So I heard this strange noise and noticed that Maizie was hanging around the cat. Well it turns out that right after tea, the cat can be sick, Maizie goes and cleans up, I witnessed this tonight. So then a little while later I heard the cat make that noise again, I got there first! When the cat is sick I now know that it is basically cat food that went into a dish, into the cat and then if I am fast enough, in to my mouth!! How epic is that, an extra meal that is slightly warmer than room temperature. Purrrrfect you could say!

For the rest of the evening I kept a very close eye on the cat but I didn't get any extra treats tonight so I just ended up going to bed.

Friday 14th December

I woke up this morning with cat food still on my mind. I went out for a wee and then settled onto the sofa for a cuddle with Mum while she had her coffee and then when she went into the bathroom I followed her out. Mum usually feeds the cat in the bathroom so I thought perhaps my luck was in. It wasn't. After Mum went to work Dad did the housework and then I decided to go out in the garden to see what I could find to do out there.

Well, I found something, the green binbag was out and it had lots of treasures in it. I emptied it out to have a look and Dad came out and caught me. I got a telling off.

After Mum came home she let us out in the garden again. I went up to the dining room window and stared into the house. I could see Mum in the dining room, she laughed at me and took a photo. What she didn't realise at the time was that I was being a look out for Rosie, she was out in the green bin looking for more treasures. I was being look out. Mum eventually worked this out and called us back in. After tea we all just cozied up in the front room for the rest of the evening and then went to bed.

Saturday 15th December

I got up later this morning. It was a really horrid day, I have never seen so much rain in my life. I quickly dashed out for a wee and then came back in for my breakfast. After breakfast I got weighed again, this week I am 21.7kg. Mum said my growth is starting to slow down and I may not get much bigger now. We will see about that.

It was raining so hard today that none of us wanted to go out at all, Mum went out and came back very wet and I didn't fancy that myself. Basically, today we just played and watched tv.

In the evening we all had a bit of a play together and even the cat joined in, I think she doesn't like getting wet either. We all chilled out in front of the tv until bed time and I was quite happy to go to bed as I have learned that the next day is the day we get a big dinner.

Sunday 16th December

I woke up this morning late again and got up on the sofa to watch Hollyoaks with Mum and Dad. I love the music so much, its brilliant and it keeps coming on every 15 minutes or so. Mum and Dad laugh at the way I stop what I'm doing to listen to the music, I really like the little twangy guitar sounding bit.

Dad went out and cooked Sunday dinner, this week we had beef. I've not had that before, Rosie and Maizie seemed very excited about this so I was too. Mum and Dad had their lunch and then Rosie and Maizie started to stretch a lot. They said it was to limber up and stretch their tummies so they could fit their dinner in. Mum gave the cat hers first I was very sad because the cat liked her beef. Last week she didn't like the pheasant so I got her share. This week I didn't.

117

Our roast was utterly fabulous. I really enjoyed it and went to see if there were any leftovers in Rosie and Maizie's dishes. There wasn't. They had eaten it all.

In the afternoon we went out for a bit but the weather was still rubbish so we all came in and lay on our blankets and dozed with our full bellies until bed time.

Monday 17th December

Today it was back to getting up early. I am getting so fed up with this awful weather, this morning everything was really slippery. The rain had stopped and it had got really cold.

I went and cuddled with Mum until she went to work and then I assisted Dad with the housework again. All day I also tried to get in the bath. This is because Dad decided that the green binbag was safer in the bath with the shower door hiding it. The shower door is so easy to open that it really didn't stop me at all. Dad was not impressed at all.

Mum came back after she had finished work and I was so excited to see her again. I wish she could stay home with me, I also think she wishes the same. She wrapped up some more boxes tonight and put then under the tree. It is getting very full under the tree now. I do keep having a good sniff to see if there is anything there for me.

After tea, we had a play around and then settled down in the front room to watch the tv, but I ended up falling asleep resting against Mum. Mum woke me up when it was time for bed. Dad let us all out and then I went in my crate. It was funny because Dad couldn't find Maizie, he looked all over the garden and then even went upstairs and asked Mum if she was up there. I knew where she was all along. She had sneaked into my crate and cuddled up with me. Dad told her that she needed to get into her own bed. I think it would have been very cozy if she had stayed with me.

Tuesday 18th December

I woke up this morning and went out for my morning wee. I got soaked again. I really don't like this time of year at all, where has the sun and warmth gone? Rosie says it will be ok and the nice days will come back. She is grown up so I suppose she knows what she is talking about.

I had my usual cuddle with Mum before she left for work and then I assisted Dad with the house work. I have realised now that the hoover is easier to attack when Dad uses it on the sofa, it's head seems to shrink then and I can get it in my mouth. It doesn't seem to kill it though. I will need to come up with a cunning plan.

Today I also got quite interested in the Christmas tree, there is a little glass thing hanging off it and I like glass. I don't understand what the fuss is about when I pick up things made of glass.

When Mum came home I got all excited again, she was carrying loads of stuff so she got a little cross at my enthusiasm. Once she put everything down I got cuddles and she tried to keep me from jumping up.

In the evening we all cosied up on the sofa and then we had an early night.

Wednesday 19ᵗʰ December

I woke up this morning and got drenched again when I went out for a wee. I came back in and went on the sofa and decided I would have a fight with my back leg. My back leg can really irritate me sometimes, it keeps kicking me in the head.

After mum went to work I helped Dad with the housework and then I got a bit bored so I decided to look and see what I could do in the garden. I found a really pretty solar light. I really likes it and it was made of glass. I bought it back into the house and sneaked into my crate with it. Dad found it and took it away, but je didn't see I had taken the post off it so I got to keep that.

When Mum came home I was so excited again, I jumped up and bit her bingo wing. She let out a scream. I didn't mean to hurt her so I tried to make up for it. I went over to give mum a cuddle and as she looked down she saw the metal post I had chewed up earlier. She picked it up and looked at it to try and work out what it was. It didn't take her long to work it out and she looked at me and told me that I need to stop doing naughty things.

I decided to have a play after tea, I was practicing my zoomies and I ended up jumping full on onto Mum's lap. My claws scratched her legs pretty badly.

After this I decided I would be a calm and good boy as I really didn't mean to hurt Mum. I got up on the sofa and cuddled Mum for the rest of the night to make up for hurting her. When Mum went to bed I went out for my wee and went to bed.

Thursday 20th December

I got up this morning and went and braved the rain to have my morning wee. I then went and cuddled up with Mum on the sofa. Mum went off to work so I had breakfast and then helped Dad with the housework. I really, very nearly got the hoover today, but it is still working so I didn't kill it properly.

It was a normal day really eat, sleep, walk, play and then it wasn't long before Mum came home. She didn't stay for long though, Dad had to go to a hospital appointment, that's why Mum came home early.

When they got back from hospital Mum went out into the garden. She looked really sad, she had found the big hole I have dug under the apple tree and also could see all the earth I have taken out of some plant pots. Apparently Mum really loves her garden so I think I am in the bad books.

To make up for this for the rest of the evening I just cuddled up with Mum on the sofa and pulled the cutest face I could so that she would not be cross with me. I was quite tired today so I decided to have an early night.

Friday 21st December

I got up this morning and went out for my usual wee, I then went and cuddled up with Mum. Things are getting very odd in the house. We have all these lights up and Rosie keeps going and looking at the stocking things that are hanging on the fireplace. There is definitely an element of excitement with everyone apart from Mum. She seems very busy and keeps wrapping things up and sometimes cries when she is doing it. It is all very weird.

I had my usual run of the mill day and then Mum came home. I was so excited again that I nipped her again. I notice now that she keeps her hand on my back and asks me not to jump up at her. It's really hard though because I like to see her face very close up when she gets home.

In the evening Mum continued wrapping stuff and then we all went in the front room to cuddle up on the sofa until bedtime.

Saturday 22nd December

This morning I got up later again as Mum was home from work. I had breakfast and then Mum did the weighing thing again. Today I am 22.2kg, Mum said it may be my last weigh in as I am now getting to heavy to pick up. I'm quite happy with that as I don't find being picked up as nice as it used to be. I used to love it, I could snuggle in and felt safe, Now I can't snuggle as I am so big I just end up sort of suspended in the air.

In the afternoon Mum and Dad went out. When they came back they had more food that I have ever seen in my little life. They obviously had a very successful hunting trip. It took them both ages to put everything away and then Mum went over and filled the stockings with what I think are dog treats and toys. Now I am starting to see why Rosie gets excited. I wonder how long they will be there before we are allowed them.

In the evening we all went into the front room to cuddle up on the blankets. Rosie couldn't settle tonight, she kept going over to the stockings and even got a bit cross when me and Maizie tried to have a sniff.

Sunday 23rd December

I woke up later this morning and then settled down to watch Hollyoaks with Mum and Dad. I love the music for that so much. I am getting the hang of things now and I understand that Sunday is a lazy day where in winter we watch tv and eat a big roast dinner. Not such a bad life really.

Mum carried on wrapping things up after lunch and the house is starting to look rather full with all these boxes everywhere. My main concern is getting the stuff that is in the stockings, I manage to get the odd occasional sniff when Rosie isn't looking because I know she will get cross with me.

For the rest of the day we chilled out with the odd occasional play. It was a pretty lovely day really and then Mum went to bed early as she has work the next day.

Monday 24th December

I woke up this morning and went and cuddled up with Mum while she had her coffee. Then when Mum went to work she took some of the parcels with her. Dad even said he would be there in a while. Dad did a bit of housework and then I went in my crate for a bit.

Dad came home first and carried on doing housework and then not long after Mum came home early. She was carrying the biggest chicken I have ever seen in my life. I really wanted it. Dad saw me sniffing it and decided it would be safer in Granny's house.

Dad went into the kitchen and started peeling vegetables, but it wasn't like the usual roast, there was enough to feed the whole street. Me and Rosie watched for ages and I could see Rosie was getting a bit excited.

In the evening I went and lay on my blankets and Rosie joined me, she put her head over my neck and fell asleep cuddling me. I am so lucky because she loves me so much. It was a lovely evening being cuddled up together. Mum and Dad went to bed quite early tonight so I got a good night's sleep.

Tuesday 25th December

122

Mum got up early and didn't get ready for work. Instead she gave us all a cuddle and said "Merry Christmas". Rosie was very hyper and excited, I really didn't have a clue what was going on. Dad got up and had a coffee and then started moving the parcels around. Mum got the stockings down and started to get the things out of them. I was right, it was lots of treats and toys for all of us. Even the cat had one.

Dad then got the giant chicken off Granny and put it in the oven. I was so excited, there would definitely be some for us dogs. There was then a knock at the door, it was Grandad and Bean and Neil. They also came with boxes but me and Rosie had to go in our crates because we were so excited. Maizie was allowed to stay out and she even had her Christmas jumper on. I was warm enough without mine.

After a while they all went in to granny's house. They also took the big chicken. This was not good. I had a nap in my crate until they all came back. The others didn't stay for long and then it was just us again. Granny passed back the big chicken and Mum made us the biggest roast we had ever had. The cat also had one.

After dinner Mum gave the cat what looked like chopped up grass, she ate it all and then started rubbing her head on the floor, then she went totally crazy and started running around and playing with her toys, I went over to see what she was doing and she chased me away.

It was a very busy day and by the evening we were all really tired. Mum went to bed as she said she had drunk too much Baileys. Rosie told me that this happens every year and I will spot the signs next year. I can't wait.

Wednesday 26th December

I woke up this morning and was very happy to see that Mum wasn't going to work again. Today is called boxing day apparently. But all the boxes were opened yesterday so to me that makes no sense. I snuggled up on the sofa for a while and then went out with Mum as she said it was warm enough to do some gardening.

At lunch time Mum took the big chicken out of the oven and started to take all the yummy meat off it. She had all these bowls and was putting different bits of meat into each of the bowls. We all hung around to watch and hope that we got some. We did, it was great, we all got a big bowl of the chicken, apparently it is actually turkey but it looks the same to me.

After lunch us dogs all went out and played chase all afternoon, we came back in doors when we were really worn out. Once we had recovered a bit, we stole all the cat's toys and played with them for the rest of the evening. It was great fun.

We then all went onto our big blanket and cuddled each other until bed time. I have had the best time ever over the last few days. I can't wait until next year as now I know what to expect.

Thursday 27th December

Well, I think things are getting back to normal now. I got up early which meant Mum was going to work today. I got up for a quick cuddle and then off she went. I had breakfast and then helped Dad with the housework.

Today was a really nice day, the sun came out and it was warm. Me, Rosie and Maizie decided to spend the day in the garden. We took all our toys out with us and basically, we played all day until it started to get dark.

Once it started to get dark, Mum came home. I was excited to see her. I do try really hard not to jump up but I just need to say hello. I had a good play with Mum and then settled down for a cuddle. Well, when I say cuddle, I really mean flop on her. I can make her groan when I do that as I am heavy now.

Mum was laughing at me tonight and saying that my coat is changing so much. Dad doesn't like it when Mum laughs at me. I was tired after my day of running about so I took myself to my crate and had an early night.

Friday 28th December

Today I got up with Mum again, she got ready for work, I went out and had a wee and then we had a cuddle before she went. Dad wasn't very well again today and he was feeling pretty rough so we amused ourselves around the house. The weather was pretty good still so we went out in the garden and enjoyed playing in the sun.

Everything is slowly getting back to normal now and it looks like there won't be anymore presents, although we now have so many toys to play with.

Mum came home at her usual time and I was really happy to see her again. I got told off again for jumping up at her, I am trying not to but it's hard as I get so excited.

In the evening we all chilled out in the front room and watched tv. I did pop out in the garden for a while and when I came back Mum saw that my beard was wet and told Dad that she thought I had been out playing in the pond. Once my beard was dry I went to bed as I was pretty tired.

Saturday 29th December

I had a lay in this morning as Mum didn't go to work. I went out for my morning wee and then had my breakfast. I got weighed again today and Mum said I weighed the same so I am slowing down now and won't get much bigger.

Mum went out in the garden and saw what I had done last night. There is a small barrel pond in the garden and it has lots of plants in it, well not anymore. Last night I had fished them all out and threw them all over the decking. Mum said some words that I can't repeat and then put all the plants back in the water and put mesh over the top. I think that is to stop me from doing that again.

In the afternoon My Mum started to do some house work so I helped, she didn't use the hoover though. Dad popped out for a while to see his friends and me and Mum then watched a film.

In the evening we watched tv and had pizza, it was very yummy and I think I could have eaten a whole one. I went to bed full of pizza and content.

Sunday 30th December

I got up this morning knowing it is Sunday. Sunday has been renamed naughty boy day. Mum and Dad say I am a pain in the bum on Sundays. We all got on the sofa to watch Hollyoaks but I ended up getting bored of that so I decided to see if the cat wanted to play with me. She didn't.

Dad cooked dinner after Hollyoaks had finished and then Mum gave us our roast dinner as per usual. Then it all got a bit odd. Mum and Dad took down the Christmas tree and all the decorations. Why did they go to all that effort only to take it all down again?

Then to add to my confusion, Mum took all the blankets out of my bed and put them all in the big machine in the kitchen. Why did she do that? My crate looked so bare, were they going to send me back to Hereford? I dd not like this one bit.

Well, it turns out that I needn't have worried, the blankets were taken out of the machine and put on the radiators, they were wet and needed to dry out.

It was a busy day with all this going on and I was very glad when it came to bed time. I was still concerned about where I was going to sleep and then Mum got all the blankets and arranged them all nicely in my crate. Yay, I got my bed back. It was wonderful, they were still warm and the smell they had was lovely. I knew I would sleep really well tonight.

Monday31st December

I got up early this morning. I am getting really confused as to what day of the week it is at the moment because Mum's routine is different. I went out for my wee and then came in for a quick cuddle with Mum before she went off to work.

Dad gave me breakfast and then did some housework. I did my best to help again and tried to kill the hoover. For most of the day it felt just like the usual day. Well, until Mum came home.

When Mum got home she had lots of bags with her and one that looked very strange as it appeared to float. She sneaked past Rosie and put the bag on the stairs, Rosie didn't see the bag.

Mum went into the bathroom and had a shower and then managed to break the bathroom window, she had to go outside to push the window shut.

After she had finished drying her hair, she poured a big drink and went into the front room. We all watched tv until Dad came home and then he started cooking really nice food. After that we all chilled out in the front room and then at bed time things started to get a bit odd.

I was ready for bed and then Mum turned the tv over, there was a big clock chiming and fireworks too. Then suddenly there were fireworks outside our house. Dad said happy new year to Mum and then they both said happy birthday to Rosie and started laughing and singing silly songs to her. She was shaking because she was a bit scared of the noises so Mum got a load of dog treats out and started to feed them to Rosie. She calmed down in the end and we all went to bed. I went into my crate and lay there wondering what the hell had gone on tonight. It was all a bit odd.

Tuesday 1st January

I got a lay in again today as Mum was home. Its all so crazy and I can't guess what day it is anymore. Mum made a coffee and then got the floaty thing out from the staircase. Mum and Dad started to sing happy birthday to Rosie and then Mum went and got three brand new big balls from the kitchen that she had hidden. They were great and smelt of beef. Yummy.

Grandad and Gran turned up too and Mum and Dad cooked another roast, we went into our crates while they ate as we were a bit excited at the day's events so far. After everyone left Dad put on a song on the Alexa thing and some man was singing "gonna party like it's your birthday" It was funny because Rosie started to twerk to it. She looked very happy.

Later on I thought I would try and make everyone laugh so I started to go out through the dog flap and go to the dining room window to look in, it really makes them laugh at me for some reason.

In the evening we were all pretty tired and Mum said she was back to work tomorrow so we all went to bed pretty early, but that was good as I was very tired.

Wednesday 2nd January

It was back to the usual routine this morning. Mum got up early and got ready for work and then we had a quick cuddle on the sofa. After Mum went Dad gave me breakfast and then did some housework. Today I couldn't be bothered to attack the hoover so I thought I would make the most of the sunshine and see what havoc I could cause outside. It was great to feel the sun on my face and actually today I thought I would be good and not wreck anything.

Rosie has been sulking all day today, Mum and Dad say it's because Rosie wanted her birthday to last longer than one day. I think her birthday was fine and I hope when mine comes that I get balloons, toys and a roast too.

The rest of the day was pretty normal really and in the evening we all settled down on the blankets while Mum and Dad watched tv. I went to bed pretty early tonight because I was still pretty tired due to everything that has been going on for the last week.

Thursday 3rd January

I got up early again today, it looks like things are getting back to normal again now. Rosie has got over sulking that it isn't her birthday anymore. I did the usual things today, I wrecked the garden a bit more, had my usual zoomie practice and harassed the other two dogs to play with me. I tried to kill the hoover once more but still failed. I noticed that mum had put wire on top of the little pond and weighed it down with a big rock. Like that was going to stop me. I don't think so. I just picked up the rock and threw it onto the decking.

When Mum got home Dad told her what I had done with the garden and she said she would go and have a proper look in the day light at the weekend.

In the evening we all played for a while and then I settled down on the sofa for a cuddle with Mum until bedtime. I went out for my last wee and then went off to bed.

Friday 4th January

I got up early with Mum again this morning, well, to be fair it did take me a while to actually get up as I was really nice and snug in my crate. I got up on the sofa and had a cuddle before she went to work and then I decided that today I was going to see just how far I could push Dad. I have decided that it is really rude to point. Mum and Dad tend to do that when they are telling me off. What I do now when they point at me is talk back. It really works, they both end up laughing at me.

Anyway, back to my day, I helped Dad with the hoovering. I have a new tactic, I now mainly attack the hoover when it has the small brush on it. I think I have a better chance with that, although today I was still unsuccessful.

Mum got home in the early evening so I jumped all over her and Mum ended up holding me down so I couldn't jump up at her. She could see how playful I was so she got my woolly ball that Parsla made me and we played together for ages. I then decided to go out through the dog flap so I could look in through the dining room window again. I really like doing that but Mum and Dad just laugh at me and wonder why I do it.

In the evening we all snugged up on our blankets and dozed until bedtime.

Saturday 5th January

I got a bit confused this morning so I alerted Mum to the fact that she needed to get up. Mum got up and then told me she wasn't going to work today. I had my breakfast and then Mum weighed me again. Today I am 23.2kg. Mum said she is really finding it hard to pick me up now and to be honest I don't really like it either. I can see all the kitchen worktops now without having to jump up. Everything looks like it is getting smaller but Mum says it's because I am getting bigger.

Mum went out in the garden and saw all the mess I had made. She spent a long time out tidying the garden and got really annoyed with me as I wanted to kill the broom. She was trying to sweep up the mess I had made and I did all I could to stop her. This resulted in me being sent back into the house and the dog flap was shut so I couldn't get out.

After Mum had used the broom I was allowed out again. I was shocked, she had covered all the plant pots in slate bits so I can't get to the earth anymore. This is not good. I need to find something else to work on in the garden now.

In the evening I was pretty tired from all the gardening so I was very happy to just sleep on the sofa cuddled up to Mum until it was time for bed.

Sunday 6th January

I woke up later this morning and was pretty confused when Mum said happy Christmas to me. Was she feeling unwell? Surely she remembers that Christmas was last week. Well it turns out that Mum's family come from a place called Ukraine and they have a different Christmas to us. There were no decoration or presents this time but Dad had bought a whole chicken. Seeing Mum doesn't eat meat I knew we were all in for a big dinner today.

I watched Hollyoaks as I love the music so much and then went and watched Dad cook dinner. It smelt wonderful and I couldn't wait to get mine. I got my dinner after Mum and Dad finished theirs. It was so tasty and we all got so much chicken. I love Sundays.

We all went out in the afternoon and ran our dinner off. I am a lot quicker than the other two dogs, they don't stand a chance of beating me anymore. In the evening we all slept on the blankets in the front room until bedtime.

I really enjoyed today, it was excellent.

Monday 7th January

Today Mum didn't go to work, I managed a good old snuggle with her this morning and then she went out. She was only gone for an hour though so that was ok. She said she had to go and have an injection. That's ok as long as I don't have to have one.

Mum and Dad then had to go out together so I went to my crate and slept until they returned. They came back empty handed, so I assumed the hunting didn't go so well today. They said they had been to hospital, and explained it was like the people version of the vets. I do hope everything is ok. I know Dad has days when he isn't well so I hope the people vet can make him better. Dad is the most important thing to me so I don't want him to be poorly.

In the evening we all snuggled down again but I kept going over to get cuddles from Dad to help make him feel better and I wanted him to see how much I love him. I think that tomorrow I am going to try really hard to be a model Pup and be the best boy I can.

Tuesday 8th January

I got up early again this morning and went out for a wee in the frost. It was very cold and slippery, so I came back in quickly and snuggled down with Mum on the sofa. After Mum went to work Dad got busy doing the housework, I went out to play rather than try and kill the hoover today, after the frost had gone it got quite nice and it was very sunny so I stayed out for ages.

I did come back in when Dad had lunch, we always sit with him when he is having lunch because we know that we will always get a bit of what he is eating.

Mum came home a bit later than usual but she had some bags with her. When she opened the bag there were loads of dog treats in it, she opened them up and gave us all a jumbone thing each. Heer trick worked because she got them to give to us to stop us jumping up at her.

It started to get cold really early today and Rosie didn't like it one bit, Mum had to wrap her up in her cardigan. At bed time Dad got the big floor blankets and put them in Rosie and Maizie's beds so they would be as snug and warm as I was.

Wednesday 9th January

I got up this morning and it was so cold. I went out and had a very quick morning wee as my feet felt so cold on the frozen decking. I wonder why it is like this now, I preferred the warm days when I was a little pup. I came back in and had a cuddle with mum and then when she got her boots out of the cupboard I inspected them to make sure there were no spiders in them, Mum was lucky as the boots were all clear of any bugs.

Mum went to work and Dad gave me breakfast and then did the housework. One the sun was up properly it wasn't too cold so I went out and started to vandalise the garden again. Mum had put stones over some of the pots to stop me eating the earth. The stones are now on the decking and I can get to the earth again until Mum notices.

When Mum came home she was talking to the neighbour, she had dropped some bags of shopping in the kitchen and told her neighbour she had to go in in case I stole it as I am now very tall. Mum opened the door and I was stood with my paws on the baby gate, the neighbour saw me and couldn't believe how big I have got. I am human size when I stand up on my back legs. Once Mum came in and settled, I went up for cuddles with her. I pretty much stayed on the sofa with Mum all evening. After she had gone to bed Dad gave me my supper but I didn't really want it. Dad was concerned that I didn't fancy my tea. I'm not sure why I didn't want it but I was ok really. I decided the best thing was to just go to bed and curl up on my blanket.

Thursday 10ᵗʰ January

I got up this morning and stayed in my crate for a while. It was all white and slippy out in the garden when I went for my wee so I didn't stay out for long. I came back in and cuddled up with Mum for a bit and put my cold feet on her to warm them up.

After breakfast, which I now find a bit dull because I would rather just have the same as the grown up dogs, I watched Dad do some repairs to the small pond as this morning I managed to trash it again and so Dad tied the mesh down this time so I can't lift it off. I was rather annoyed by this to be honest.

When Mum got home I was really excited again and after jumping up at her a few times she got some treats and made me sit. Well of course I will if I am going to get food. Dad said that he thought I was getting bored of puppy food so Mum suggested we just do half puppy and half adult, I am very happy with this solution.

In the evening we all cuddled up together on the blankets and Rosie kept me lovely and warm until bed time.

Friday 11ᵗʰ January

I woke up this morning and went out into the cold for my morning wee. It was really cold again. I came back in and cuddled up with Mum on the sofa while she drank her coffee and got ready to go to work. After my breakfast I assisted Dad with his chores and then went out in the garden to play for a while with the other two dogs. We didn't stay out so long today and thought it would be far nicer to play indoors where we have the soft blankets to land on when we play.

It was a usual day really until Mum came home. She looked really tired tonight, she had had a tough day at work. Mum keeps saying she wishes she could retire and stay at home. We would all like that too. It would be great if we were all together all the time.

In the evening, Mum played with us and then we all got tired so we all went to sleep on the sofa and Maizie went and slept on the blanket. We went to bed quite early tonight as we were all so tired.

Saturday 12th January

Mum didn't go to work today so we all stayed in bed a bit longer than usual. Mum must have been really tired. I had my breakfast and then was weighed again. Today I was 23.4kg so I haven't put much weight on this week. Mum said that she thinks I will stay around the size I am now.

Mum went out to do some gardening and I helped her with it. I think she got annoyed as she then gave up and we went back in doors.

Dad got a bag ready and I got the feeling he was going to go away. I was right, at teatime he went out. Mum put the tv on and we all slept while she watched films. I don't like it when Dad goes away, I really miss him and to be fair, when Mum cooks herself tea it is usually something really rubbish and even if she offered us some we wouldn't want it.

Later on she started to talk to her computer, it was very weird because I could hear someone talking back to her. It was her friend Banf. He started to call me so I got right in Mum's way and all he could see was me moving my head around to get my ears to pick up the sound better, they were both laughing. Mum talked to Banf on the computer for ages and then in the end said she was very tired and needed to go to bed.

She let us all out and then we all got ready for bed. Dad still wasn't home. I really hope he is back tomorrow. I miss him so very much.

Sunday 13th January

Today I woke up later but Mum was still asleep so I barked to wake her up. She got up and let me out for a wee, I was really glad as I needed to go badly. She didn't do the usual routine of putting Hollyoaks on and Dad still wasn't back. I really wanted him to come home as it was roast day and we didn't want to miss out.

Later on in the morning Rosie and Maizie got really excited, they had heard Dad's car, he was back. I was so excited I nearly did a wee. Dad gave me a massive hug and then after a cup of tea, he started to cook roast, we all went outside and ran up and down the garden until we had got over our excitement.

Roast was lovely today, I got loads of chicken. It's really yummy and I like it a lot. For the rest of the day all we did was pretty much sleep as we were all so worried about Dad going missing yesterday that we didn't really sleep. We were all very tired and I was very glad to have an early night tonight.

Monday 14th January

I woke up this morning and went out for a wee, it wasn't so cold today so I had a quick scan of the garden to make sure everything was ok. I then came back in and had my morning cuddle with Mum. I have had a major discovery lately, I see Rosie does this weird dance when Mum scratches her back for her, she calls it twerking. Well, I get it now, having a back scratch is just the best thing ever, mind you saying that having any form of physical contact is great, I also really like being stroked on my head and around my ears.

Dad spent most of the day cleaning the kitchen while I worked out a few new things for myself. I have been watching the way Mum and Dad open the back door, I noticed that they push the handle thing down. I can reach it quite easily with my mouth but I had problems getting a grip of it with my teeth. I will practice that a bit more. Dad eventually worked out what I was trying to do as the door handle was all wet by the time I finished

In the evening I cuddled Mum, played with Rosie and got a shoulder massage from Dad and that fab back rub from Mum. Getting older doesn't seem so bad really.

Tuesday 15th January

I woke up this morning and went out for my usual wee. I then came back in and cuddled up with Mum, I was really awake this morning so I decided I wanted to play with Mum, but she really wanted to sit calmly and just have her morning coffee.

When Mum had gone to work Dad gave me my breakfast, he is starting to mix my puppy food with the other dogs stuff, this makes me very happy as I really like it. I'm liking lots of things at the moment. I especially like being stroked and cuddled. I also want to be brushed I think. Mum said she will get me one.

In the afternoon I went out to see what I could wreck in the garden. I decided today it would be the fig tree, it now just looks like a chewed up branch, I'm hoping Mum doesn't notice what I have done for a while.

When Mum came home II jumped all over her so she went into the kitchen and bribed me to stop by giving me biscuits. I ate the biscuits and continued to jump around for a while longer. Eventually I did calm down and cuddled up with Mum on the sofa until it was time for bed. I went into my crate and snuggled down on my blankets.

Wednesday 16th January

I got up this morning and it was chucking it down with rain. I didn't stay out for long and then came in for my morning cuddles. Mum looked annoyed that it was raining but said she was happy that she didn't have to de ice the car. I liked it because the garden wasn't slippery.

Dad did loads of housework today, he kept himself busy, it wouldn't stop raining so there was no chance of him getting any of us to go out today. I kept myself amused by playing with Maizie and then I tucked into my antler. It has taken me ages to try and eat it and I haven't even made a dent in it.

Mum came home and said she was very sore but I didn't understand. I jumped up at her and she kept saying ouch. She had a deep tissue massage what ever that is. Eventually I calmed down and had a good play with Mum and the other dogs. It was a quiet evening really. Well, until Dad had his shower. Apparently he never had the dogs come in when he was having a shower, now he has to put up with me. He started to laugh and say now as I managed to lick one of his bum cheeks. When he got out of the shower I also helped by drying one of his legs for him.

After Dad's shower I went back in the front room and listened to Dad letting Mum how much he loves me. I went off to bed a very happy boy tonight.

Thursday 17ᵗʰ January

 Woke up this morning feeling like I am the man. I went out for a quick wee and then decided that I was going to get behind Mum on the sofa and bit her bum and then try and push her off the sofa, I then started playing the bitey game. When Dad got up, Mum told him I was full of attitude today. I'm just confident that's all. Although to be fair today I felt that I would see how far I could assert my authority.

I annoyed Dad a great deal today and he was starting to get a bit fed up with me. Dad ended up going out just before Mum got home.

When Mum got home I jumped all over her, she opened the back door to let me out and noticed that I had chewed one of her trees, she moved it onto the table to stop me chewing it and went back indoors. A while later she came back out again and shouted at me. I had knocked over a big plant pot with a banana tree in it, I wanted to see what was buried in there so I pulled out all the earth and spread it all over the decking to see if I could find anything. Mum went and got a broom and tried to sweep it all up and then I grabbed the end of the broom so she couldn't sweep up.

Granny came out and grabbed hold of me so that Mum could sweep up and re pot the banana.

When Dad came home he saw a photo of the mess and said that I had been naughty all day. Mum said she had worked that out. After tea Mum went in for a bath, I went in to watch and once she was properly in the water, I picked up her pants and ran around the house, throwing them in the air. When she got out of the bath I dried one of her legs for her before she got dressed.

I did eventually chill out and went and nicely cuddled up with Mum because I knew she wouldn't be able to stay cross at my little puppy face. I was pretty glad to get to bed tonight as all the naughtiness had made me very tired.

Friday 18th January

I woke up this morning and yet again was full of trouble. I went out for my wee and then went and cuddled Mum and played with her hand. I like to still bite it but I am very gentle when I do it still. Dad gave me my breakfast and then I went to help him with the hoovering. I didn't like it so much today, it smelt really odd and I got the sense of danger from it.

I went out to see if I could kill the banana tree again today but Mum had put a barrier right in front of all the plant pots so I couldn't reach it. I was most annoyed.

The rest of the afternoon was the same old routine, exercise, play, sleep eat and then Mum came home. I was so excited to see Mum. I jumped all over her again. I eventually calmed down and then listened to Dad telling Mum about the hoover. Apparently the smell it made was because it's dying. Yay, I finally did it, I killed it at last.

In the evening we all went into the front room and chilled out. I played for a bit and then cuddled up with Mum on the sofa until bedtime. I was pleased again to get to bed tonight.

Saturday 19th January

I woke up this morning and was a bit confused as Mum was in her work clothes. We still managed to have our morning cuddle though and she didn't go as early as she usually does. Mum gave me breakfast and then weighed me. I was 23.6kg this week so I have only put on a little bit of weight this week.

When Mum went out I played with the other two dogs and then there was a knock at the door. It was a man who gave Dad a massive box. What was in the box I wondered. Well, I could have screamed. Dad pulled out this big round thing with a long tube and a long wire, he put it all together and then plugged it in. It was another hoover. I couldn't believe it. It was even bigger than the last one. As soon as Dad turned it on I went for it. I tried to kill it but it is way stronger than the last one.

Mum eventually came home and then we played for a while. Dad was getting ready to go out by the look of it. After a while, Jamie and Parsla came over and took Dad with them. I am really glad that they didn't take Mum with them. Mum told us that Dad wouldn't be too long and that she wanted to watch some scary films while Dad was out. Well, we all decided to go to sleep and let her watch tv in peace. It was funny because I woke up and Mum had fallen asleep.

Dad came home pretty early, but he really didn't look very well. Dad has a kidney problem and it can make him very sick sometimes. He was really sick tonight and I felt really sorry for him. Before I went to bed tonight I gave him a massive cuddle to try and make him feel better. I really he feels better tomorrow.

Sunday 20th January

I woke up this morning still worried about Dad. Mum got up and let us out for a wee and didn't look overly concerned so I was hoping Dad was better. After a while Dad came down and he looked ok. I was so happy so I got up on his lap for a cuddle. I was so happy he was better.

We watched Hollyoaks again and Mum and Dad laughed at me when the music came on. After they finished watching that, Dad started to get the dinner ready, this really is the best day of the week. I love getting a chicken dinner.

While we were waiting for dinner I had a play with the cat, she sits on the table and tries to catch my nose with her knife hands. She ended up getting really brave and started to chase me around the house. Lunchtime came and we all had our dinner, I do think it's a bit unfair that the cat gets hers first though.

In the afternoon Mum didn't look so well. What is it with humans? I know there are lots of things happening at the moment and Mum seems to be working more so perhaps that is all that is wrong.

We didn't really do much for the rest of the day apart from eat, sleep and play occasionally. Mum and Dad went to bed quite early tonight and I was also happy to get to bed.

Monday 21st January

I got up with Mum again this morning, she left a little bit earlier today as she said she had a lot to do. I wish she could stay home more as she goes out nearly every day. After she left, Dad gave us breakfast and then got that hoover out again. Well I tried to kill it again. I will not give in.

It was a usual day, same old routine, eat, sleep, walk, play and then go to the garden and see what I can do out there to make it better. I amused myself until Mum came home. I did the usual excited thing and she kept pushing me down and saying no. Once I stopped jumping up at her I got a biscuit. I call that bribery really.

In the evening Mum was pretty tired so she went in for a bath and after I helped her to dry off we both cuddled up together until bedtime. She went to bed early again today, but I really don't mind that.

Tuesday 22nd January

I got up early with Mum again this morning. I went out for my wee and then cuddled up with Mum until she went to work. Dad then gave me breakfast and let me out in the garden to play.

I stayed out there for a while and then was called back in. I was gutted as I was busy playing in the little pond again. Apparently he sent me out to play so I wouldn't hear the hoover. It got away today and gets to live another day.

It was another normal day but very cold and we didn't want to go out. We all snuggled up and had a lazy day on the sofa seeing no one else was using it.

When Mum came home we all got excited and went with her to the kitchen as we have worked out she gives us biscuits straight away now so we forget to jump up at her.

I helped Mum have a bath in the evening and then we all chilled out in the front room until bed time. Today was pretty uneventful really, but that isn't always a bad thing.

Wednesday 23rd January

I got up with Mum today and went out for a wee. I came back in and had a cuddle and then just before Dad got up I went back outside again. I found a little patch of earth that I felt needed to be dug over. I heard dad get up from outside so I came back in through the dog flap to say hi and both Mum and Dad started shouting don't move. They got a towel and started to rub my feet. I looked around and could see that I had left muddy footprints everywhere.

After my feet were cleaned I decided I had better try to be good. I went and had a nap for a while and then I was back in Dad's good books so I helped him with the hoovering again.

I was a good boy for the rest of the day today, I like it when I am good as it makes Mum and Dad very happy.

In the evening I had lots of cuddles and snuggled up on the sofa with Mum until we went to bed.

Thursday 24th January

I got up this morning and it was raining again. I really wish those happy, sunny days would come back. I dashed out for a quick wee and then went and inspected Mum's work boots. She keeps pushing me away when she puts them on as she says I may get my beard caught in the zip. She doesn't understand I only look to make sure they are safe for her to put on. After Mum went to work, Dad gave me breakfast and then I helped with the hoovering again. It was so horrible outside that none of us wanted to go out at all today so we had a play in the house and then slept for most of the afternoon.

Mum came home and as I jumped up at her I caught her arm with my claws. I really didn't mean to hurt her. She said she is covered in bruises from me and I am a big doofus. I don't know what that means.

In the evening I had a play with Mum and then we all cuddled up together on the sofa until bedtime.

Friday 25th January

This morning was another damp day, and it was cold too. I went and had my wee and then came right back in again. I really am getting fed up with this weather now. I came back in and had big cuddles with Mum and inspected her boots again. She does seem to find this quite funny.

Mum went to work so Dad did the hoovering and started to clean out the kitchen. I stayed very close to him all afternoon as the kitchen is where all the food is kept and I thought I may get a snack out of it.

Mum was sad when she came home, Jamie's mum went to heaven yesterday, she said she felt sorry for all the family, but she told me that she will now see all the pet dogs she had in her life and they will all be

142

back together now forever. I like the thought of that. I hope it is nice and sunny where they are so they can all play outside.

In the evening I watched Mum have a bath, while she wasn't looking I stole her pants and took them to my bed. When she got out of the bath she came and got them back. Am I not allowed anything to play with? I got quite tired so I went and cuddled up with Mum until bedtime.

Saturday 26th January

I got up late this morning as it is the thing called the weekend. I love it. Mum and Dad are home for these days. I went out for a wee and then started to hassle Mum for breakfast. I ate my breakfast and then she weighed me again. She can just about pick me up now. My weight remained the same as last week at around 23.5kg. It looks like I am pretty much as big as I am going to get.

It rained all day again today so we just stayed in and played for a bit. Mum was really tired and slept most of the day and fell asleep again in the evening. I think she is really busy and this makes her tired. She said she hates January.

It started to get quite windy in the evening so we all snuggled up in the warm and dry and watched tv until bedtime.

Sunday 27th January

I got up and was really tired this morning. The sound of the wind kept me awake for most of the night. Mum went out before we were allowed for a wee as she was worried the fence may have blown over. Luckily it hadn't so we were allowed out for a wee. The cover had come off the swing last night and there was rubbish and leaves blowing everywhere. I didn't like the wind as it went in my ears and I couldn't hear properly.

Dad got up and I knew it was roast day today. It's so yummy. I love Sundays. I listened to my favorite Hollyoaks music and watched Dad cook

143

dinner. He gave us raw carrot while we watched, I really liked that, it was very crunchy.

Mum made our lunch once she had done the dishes and then we were all full and fat. I decided I wanted a cuddle with Mum so I threw myself at her. She helped me get comfy on her lap and laughed at me. She called me that doofus name again.

We all cuddled up and had the most lazy day today, the weather was so awful and I really don't like the wind. I was glad to go to bed tonight and get some proper sleep.

Monday 28th January

I got up this morning and went out for a wee. It wasn't raining and it wasn't windy. I was so glad about this. I inspected Mum's boots and then watched her take her bags and go to work. Dad gave me my breakfast and I loved it. I am gradually getting the same to eat as the other two dogs. Dad said it's the last pack of puppy meat today so I suppose tomorrow I will officially be a big boy.

The weather was fab today. I spent all day playing and running around, it was great to run like the wind. I hate it when it rains as I don't like going out in it so today was perfect.

Mum got home and we went outside to see what proper damage the storm had caused. She looks sad when she looks at the garden as she doesn't like how I have damaged it. All I have done is dig a few holes to be fair.

In the evening I was really tired so I just cuddled up with Rosie on the blankets and dozed until it was time for bed.

Tuesday 29th January

I got up this morning and was rather hungry so I tried to get into the cupboard under the stairs where Mum and Dad keep the dog food. I couldn't open it so I went outside and dug a big hole in the garden.

Nobody noticed so I got away with it yet again. It was quite cold today so I didn't really go out much, I curled up on the blanket to keep warm and comfy.

Dad noticed my big hole in the end and was very annoyed, this was because I had popped out again to go to the loo and when I came back in there were muddy footprints all over the kitchen floor.

I tried to cheer Dad up by helping to kill the hoover again and it worked, making him laugh is the best way to get out of trouble.

In the evening Mum came home and we all just chilled out for the rest of the evening. Mum wasn't her usual self tonight and I went to bed wondering what was going on.

Wednesday 30th January

Mum got up in the morning and we all went out for a quick wee. The decking was so cold and very slippery, I didn't like it as my feet got really cold. I came back in and rested my paws on Mum's back to get them warm again.
When Dad got up we had breakfast and then Mum and Dad both went out in Mum's car. About an hour later Dad came home but Mum wasn't with him. I didn't understand what was going on as Dad had Mums car.

Dad kept me busy today and I helped with the chores until I got tired. Then later on Dad asked me to go to bed and went out again. When he came back he had Mum with him, I was so happy. She told me to be careful because she had sore arms. Apparently she had lots of blood tests today and I heard her tell Dad it was very boring.

In the evening I cuddled up with Mum and looked after her. I stayed on the sofa with her until bedtime. It was really cold again tonight and I saw a few bits of white stuff fall from the sky. It looked like feathers to me.

Thursday 31st January

I got up again with Mum and got the feeling today was going to be different too. I was right. I had breakfast and then Mum and Dad went out to the car. I went to sleep for the morning as there was nothing to do with them both out.

They came home around lunchtime and had lots of shopping with them. Mum was laughing with Dad as apparently, she had to go a wee in front of someone today. I can't see what is so funny as I wee in front of people all the time. It was really cold again today and the decking stayed slippery all day. I didn't want to go out and get me feet cold and neither did Rosie so we curled up together to keep warm.

Mum got a bit sad tonight, she said it was because it was Zak's birthday and he is at rainbow bridge so she can't give him hugs, kisses and presents anymore. I think she still misses him very much.

In the evening when it was time for bed, Dad got the big blankets out and put them in our beds. It was so lovely and snug. I couldn't wait to go to bed tonight with all the extra blankets.

Friday 1st February

I got up today at the usual time with Mum. It was still really cold and slippery outside. I hate it. I came back in and warmed my feet up on Mum again until she went to work. Dad gave me my breakfast this morning and then I went out to play on the slippy decking again until my feet couldn't stand it anymore. Neither of the other two would join my though so it was a bit boring.

I then went and assisted Dad with the housework and tried yet again to kill the hoover. Yet again I failed. I don't get why Dad laughs, does he not realise I am trying to save him from that horrible monster.

When Mum came home she had lovely treats with her. She gave us all a big jumbone each. I love them, they are so yummy. Later on we all chilled out in the front room and Mum started to laugh, she showed Dad a picture on her computer. It was lots of Dogs who had their privates covered in glitter, glitter balls they are called, well they can forget that. I wont let them do that to me.

146

I went to bed tonight with my bits tucked in as I didn't want to wake up in the morning with colourful, glittery balls thank you very much.

Saturday 2nd February

Today when I got up it wasn't as cold. It was just raining instead. I just want to be warm and to be able to sit in the sun like I used to when I was little.

Mum gave me breakfast and weighed me. My weight has been the same for 3 weeks now. I am 23kg. Mum seems to think I have nearly finished getting as big as I am going to. I don't mind that though as I don't want me bed to get any smaller.

In the afternoon I got into trouble again. I went out and carried on digging my hole. Then I saw the other dogs go back in doors so I ran really fast back into the house and did a massive skid in the front room. Mum looked horrified, I had left big streaks of mud on the carpet. Mum got some spray out and started to clean the carpet. The stuff smelt lovely but she kept pushing me away from it.

For the rest of the day I thought I would be good so I played with the new woolly balls that Parsla had made for us. She made us loads and they are our favourite toys.

In the evening we watched tv and all cuddled up together until it was time for bed.

Sunday 3rd February

I had a lay in this morning and then got up eventually. It's my best day of the week. We sat and watched Hollyoaks again and Mum and Dad still laugh at me every time I hear the music. I love it. It is such a catchy tune and makes my ears tingle. Dad popped out after Hollyoaks and I got a bit worried for a minute as he usually starts to cook our roast right after. It was ok though because Mum started cooking and then Dad came back after about 15 minutes and took over.

We had a great big chicken dinner each and then Dad was showing something to Mum on the computer. He has found a private field that he can take us to. He said now I am bigger he wants to see me run properly. I'm not allowed off the lead in the park as Mum and Dad say I may hurt someone if I run into them. I would only run into someone if they were stupid though and get in my way. The other dogs didn't hear what Mum and Dad were talking about so I am going to keep t as a surprise for them.

In the evening we all relaxed in front of the tv until bedtime. I went to bed dreaming of running as fast as I can in a big wide field. I am so excited.

Monday 4th February

I woke up this morning and went right outside, it was very wet out but it was so much warmer this morning. I was really pleased with this so I stayed out for a while and inspected the garden. I didn't cause any damage though and I knew I had about half hour of cuddles with Mum until she had to go to work.

Dad gave us breakfast and then I helped him with the housework for a bit. He then popped out and came home with his car, it had been to the car doctor. The car is ok which I am happy about as we are going on our field trip tomorrow. I am quite excited about that. Dad said it will rain tomorrow but I don't care about that. Rosie won't like it though. She hates getting wet.

Mum came home and I jumped all over her, she now gives me a chew as soon as she gets into the kitchen as that then stops me. I can lick her face now when I stand up like a person. I am a very tall Pup now.

In the evening I played with Maizie for a bit, then played with the cat who got really cross with me so in the end I got onto the sofa and cuddled up with Mum and Rosie until it was time for bed.

Tuesday 5th February

148

I woke up this morning and it was misty and raining. I didn't stay out for long and went and had a cuddle with Mum before she went to work. I then had breakfast and Dad took us all out to the car.

I haven't been in the car with the other two since I was bought home from Hereford so I was a bit confused as to what was going on. Dad drove into a big field and then opened the boot. We all jumped out and realised we could run as much as we wanted.

It was great, I ran and ran and loved it. Maizie and Rosie were running around like lunatics too and had a brilliant time. Suddenly it all went wrong. Maizie nipped Rosie's back leg and Rosie told Maizie off, with that Maizie bit Rosie on the head. It was awful. There was blood everywhere. Dad put us all in the car and took us home.

When we got home Dad cleaned Rosie's head and then took her to the vets. She came back and all was ok. I was so confused as to why this happened. We all get along so well and I actually felt quite frightened. Dad said it was because he forgot to take the muzzle. See, the problem is that lurchers get very excited when running and Dad says that's why they wear muzzles, so they can't hurt each other. Dad told me not to worry.

When Mum came home she saw Rosie's head and felt sad. Rosie stuck to her like glue all evening. Dad told Mum he is going to make sure we all have muzzles for our next trip to the field and I am glad he hasn't decided not to take us anymore. At least next time we can all run and play and no one will get hurt.

We all snuggled down in the front room tonight, it had been a very tiring and worrying day and I was very glad to go to bed tonight. That field was brilliant though and I can't wait until next time.

Wednesday 6th February

I woke up this morning and the first thing I wanted to do was to check Rosie was ok. I gave her head a sniff and she wagged her tail at me. She looked a lot better this morning and Maizie was also fine. Yesterday was horrid so I was hoping for a much better day today.

149

I had a cuddle with Mum before she went to work and then had breakfast. Today we didn't go out so I spent my day playing in the garden and playing with Maizie. I didn't play with Rosie today in case I caught her sore face so when I got tired I went and curled up on the sofa with her and we cuddled up together.

I did my usual chores today and yet again I tried in vain to kill the hoover. One day I will do it.

Mum came home and gave Rosie a cuddle. I kept jumping up at Mum and she kept telling me not to. After I calmed down I went outside so I could look in through the dining room window. I love doing this because it makes Mum and Dad laugh so much. In the evening Mum had a bath, I stole her pants again and took them to bed with me.

We all watched the tv for the rest of the evening and I went to bed a lot happier tonight.

Thursday 7th February

I woke up this morning and it was blowing a gale and raining hard. I hate this weather so much. I just want the sun to shine and be out doors on the lovely swing seat. I had a very quick wee and then went in for Mummy cuddles before she went to work. Rosie was much better today and wanted to play. I was still very careful to not hurt her sore face.

Dad was busy today, he did the housework and then went out to do what I call hunting. He is really good at it. He goes out and comes back with so many nice things, including treats for us. I think it's funny because Mum goes out all day for ages and hardly ever brings anything home. I guess she just isn't as good as Dad at hunting.

I had a nice afternoon dosing in my crate and then Mum came home. It had stopped raining so I went out and had a bit of a play and then started to chase my willy again. Mum gets really annoyed when I do it because she says I have hurt it before as I bit it too hard. She called me in and gave me a toy to play with instead.

In the evening Dad bought down a nice new blanket from upstairs because the ones we used to have are in our beds to keep us warm at night. It was a really lovely soft blanket so we all went and lay on it for the evening while Mum and Dad watched tv.

It started to get really windy again tonight so I was really glad to go into my crate and lock out the world outside and go to sleep.

Friday 8th February

I woke up this morning and it was still really windy, it was even worse than yesterday. I went out for a very quick wee and then came right back in for cuddles with Mum. I stuck around with Mum until she got ready for work and then waited for Dad to give us breakfast. It was a really horrible day today and none of us fancied going out at all.

I helped Dad with the housework and then had a play with Maizie. Rosie still has a sore head so I thought I would leave her alone so she can get better quicker.

We didn't really do much today, when Mum came home we had a play and then just all chilled out in the front room and watched tv until bedtime. I just hope the wind stops overnight as I really don't like it at all.

Saturday 9th February

I got up later today as Mum was not at work. Aunty Bean came to see us this morning and we were all really excited. She had bought a big long white dress with her. She is getting married soon.

After she went Mum went to the shops and came back with food and dog treats. We each had a big chew and it was yummy. Then the weekend went a bit strange. Rosie came out of her crate when she finished her chew and she had a big lump on her head where the bite was. She started to shake and wasn't happy at all. Then it popped. There was blood

151

everywhere. Mum cleaned her up and sat with her all evening to keep cleaning her head and give her cuddles. 7

Dad went to bed and Mum got a blanket and lay on the sofa with Rosie, they didn't sleep all night. Poor Rosie looked very sorry for herself. Later on in the night Rosie was sick, Mum cleaned it up and then got back on the sofa, I tried to get on there too but there wasn't enough room for all three of us so I had a bit of blanket on the floor under Rosie and Mum and that did me fine. I managed to doze off eventually.

Sunday 10th February

I woke up and noticed Mum and Rosie were still on the sofa. When Dad got up Mum said she was going to ring the vet. The vet said to bring Rosie in so Mum put her in the car and off they went.

When Mum came home I was shocked. Rosie had her head shaved and there was blood all over her head. The vet had to clean her wound and then had to squeeze lots of blood out of it. Mum came home with lots of medicine and some yellow stuff to clean Rosie's head with.

I was still so tired from yesterday so for the rest of the day I slept. Rosie stayed with Mum all day so she could look after her. Her poor head looked so sore but at least she felt better enough to sleep now.

We all slept into the evening and then when it was time for bed Mum went upstairs and Dad stayed up for the night to carry on looking after Rosie. This weekend has been pretty rubbish. I hope Rosie gets better soon so we can all get back to normal.

Monday 11th February

I woke up this morning on a blanket as I didn't sleep in my crate last night, I slept with Dad and Rosie in the front room. Mum came downstairs and told Dad to go to bed for a bit so he did. This morning Mum gave us breakfast, she had to hide some tablets in Rosie's food. She forgot to tell

Dad though that we had been fed so after she went to work it was brilliant because we got fed again.

Mum came home again later in the morning to look after Rosie. She sat with her all day and then at tea time she took her out to the car. I know she isn't feeling well and I was really worried. About an hour later they came home and Rosie had this big, silly pot thing on her head. I thought she looked really funny but she didn't seem to mind it. Mum then gave us our tea and hid more meds in Rosie's food, which had been mashed up.

In the evening we all chilled out in the front room and I got up on the sofa to keep Rosie company and to look after her. At bed time we all went into our beds and Rosie seemed happy in her crate with her cone on. Mum and Dad both went to bed tonight so at least things were a bit back to normal again.

Tuesday 12th February

This morning I got up with Mum and then went over to Rosie right away to see how she was. Rosie looked a lot better this morning and there was none of that red stuff coming out of her head. Mum said that Dad would have to monitor her today as the vet wanted to know how she was.

We had a quiet day today as we wanted to all keep Rosie calm. So I had a quick play with Maizie when Rosie was asleep and then I cuddled up with Rosie on the sofa so I could make sure she was ok.

Dad did housework and then went out for a while. We all slept while he was gone and when we woke up again Rosie still looked ok.

Mum came home from work and told us that she had sent photos of Rosie's head to the vet and they agreed that she didn't need to go back today and that staying calm would be better for her. She is funny as she really doesn't seem to mind wearing the plant pot thing on her head. In fact when she eats her tea none of us can try and steal it as the pot covers the whole dish.

In the evening Rosie cuddled up with Mum and there was room for me too so we all cuddled up on the sofa until it was time to go to bed. I fell much happier today seeing Rosie being more like herself again.

Wednesday 13th February

I woke up this morning and checked Rosie was ok, I went out for my wee and I couldn't believe it, Rosie managed to get out of the dog flap wearing that plant pot. I wish I had seen how she did it, I turned around and there she was. We went back in and had cuddles with Mum until she went to work.

Dad did the housework as usual and gave us breakfast, we was really concerned as we didn't eat much. What he didn't know was that because Mum is giving Rosie medication, she fed us all before Dad got up. I think I may be even heavier by the weekend with my extra food. I managed to attack the hoover again today and then played with Maizie.

The sun came out so I went to play in the garden. We are under house arrest at the moment as Mum and Dad are still trying to keep Rosie calm due to her sore head. I didn't mind though, I ran around the garden until I got really tired.

In the evening when Mum got home we all chilled out in the front room and watched tv until bedtime. Rosie stayed cuddled up on Mums lap all evening. We all went to bed and cuddled up in our blankets quite early tonight but I didn't mind that at all.

Thursday 14th February

This morning I woke up and Rosie came to see me. She still has the plant pot on but looked a lot happier today. I saw her go through the dog flap this morning, she bowed her head down and twisted the cone through the dog flap. I wonder if I will ever learn tricks like that. Mum fed us again and put medication in Rosie's food. Rosie has to have soft food at the moment as the vet said she doesn't want her chewing much still.

Dad got up and then Mum went to work. I helped with the housework and then went out to play for most of the day. Rosie came out a few times and joined in but Dad called her back every time and said she still needs to be careful.

Today is Valentine's day, apparently, it's the day people say I love you a lot. But shouldn't that be every day? Mum bought home a bottle of posh wine and put a heart on it with a note that said it was from all us dogs. I love Dad so I am glad she did that.

The house smelled lovely as Dad had cooked Mum's favourite tea for her. I like Valentines day I have decided.

In the evening we all cuddled up together and then I decided to sleep on Mum's lap. I don't fit on there as well as I used to but it was still ok. Dad thought it was funny and took a photo. Rosie was much better today and slept on the blanket as she didn't need so many cuddles today.

We all went to bed early again today and curled up in our lovely blankets.

Friday 15th February

I got up with Mum this morning and went out to the garden. When I came back in the cat decided that she wanted to play. Mum gets very worried about this as the cat is really old and I am really big. Mum told me to stop so eventually after the cat made me cry I decided to do as I was told.

Mum went off to work and I helped Dad do the housework. We had only just finished this and to my surprise Mum came home. She gave us all a quick cuddle and then had a shower. It was a bit odd as she dressed in the sort of clothes she wore when I first came here. All her clothes were very light in colour.

After she was ready Mum and Dad both went out so we all curled up and went to sleep. They had gone to say goodbye to Jamie's Mum. She had been very poorly and went over to rainbow bridge. That is very sad and I wouldn't want my Mum or Dad going there as I would miss them.

They didn't stay out too long and we were all really happy to see Mum and Dad when they came back. They gave us our tea and then we all cuddled up together for the evening. It was such a lovely and warm day today that I went to bed dreaming of those long and hot sunny days of my puppyhood.

Saturday 16th February

I got up later today as Mum wasn't going to work. I went out into the garden and was really annoyed. It was raining. Mum was really annoyed too as she said yesterday we would spend the day in the garden today. Well, I wasn't up for going out there and getting wet, it make's all my fur go curly when I get wet.

Mum helped Dad tidy up today and then when Dad did the hoovering Mum laughed when she watched me try to kill the hoover again. We didn't really do very much at all today and Rosie is still not quite herself.

In the evening we all watched tv in the front room and were lucky enough to get a bit of pizza each. We had a fairly early night tonight but I didn't mind.

Sunday 17th February

I woke up this morning and it was still raining a bit. I wasn't very impressed at all. We had breakfast and then Hollyoaks came on the tv. I really love the music on that and really look forward to Sundays as it's the best dinner day of the week.

Dad got dinner ready and then to my surprise Grandad came over. I usually go into my crate when he comes as he is quite old and Mum and Dad don't want me to hurt him by accident. Just as dinner was ready, Granny came in from next door. They all ate dinner and we all waited patiently for ours.

Mum prepared our dinner after they had all finished. I had my first ever, proper grown up roast. I got a bit excited about this and did something I haven't done since I was a little pup. I weed myself. Mum was shocked and said I did a bigger wee than most people would. She cleaned it up and all was good.

After everyone went we carried on watching the tv. It stopped raining for a while so we all went out. That was really good.

We all lazed around in the evening and then all went to bed rather early and I went into my crate and snuggled down with my blankets.

Monday 18th February

I woke up this morning and cuddled up with Mum until she was ready to go to work. When Dad got up he looked a bit poorly and was sneezing a lot. Mum went off to work as usual and I helped Dad with the housework. I tried to get Rosie to play with me but she wasn't too keen, she still has the big pot on her head and still quite quiet.

It was a pretty usual day and Mum came home and I played with her a lot. We all went out and had a great time as Maizie had found the brilliant blue ball that we all played with when I was little.

After tea, I was quite tired. I played with the cat for a while and then was pretty grateful to go to bed.

Tuesday 19th February

I got up this morning and went out for a wee before coming back in and cuddling up with Mum. When Dad got up he looked very poorly and we were all really concerned. Mum went off to work and then Dad gave us breakfast and then he went and lay down on the sofa. This isn't like Dad, we usually do the housework and I fight the hoover. Dad stayed on the sofa for most of the day so I played with Maizie and the cat and then cuddled up with him.

Mum came home and could see Dad was poorly, she had bought him some medicine to try and make him better. I do hope it works. I don't like seeing Dad poorly, especially as Rosie is still in her plant pot thing too.

Mum fed us all tonight and played with us. My heart wasn't really in it though as I was far too worried about Dad. We all had a big cuddle on the sofa and then had an early night. I could hear Dad coughing all night upstairs. This made me sad.

Wednesday 20th February

I woke up a bit later this morning and sounded the alarm. It was 7am and Mum wasn't up yet. She came and let me out for a wee and then I realised that she was going to stay at home today. She looked quite tired.

Dad woke up and came down, today he looked really poorly and we were all really worried. He has something called the flu Mum said. But he also is poorly with his kidneys too so that's why it hit him so hard.

Mum did all the housework today and looked after Dad, she went to the shops and got more cough sweets for Dad and then started to wash all our dog beds. Later on we all went outside and stayed out for ages, it was good to get the fresh air but I was still worried about Dad and didn't want to stay out.

Mum also decided today that Rosie could have the plant pot off. I was so pleased with this and so was Rosie. She rubbed her head loads on the blankets and then invited me to have a play with her. It was brilliant as I have missed playing with her.

In the evening I cuddled up with Dad to try and make him feel better. Mum put all our nice clean blankets in our beds and we all went to bed with lovely smells coming from our beds. I really hope Dad is feeling better tomorrow.

Thursday 21st February

This morning when I got up Mum looked very tired. I went out for a wee and then had a cuddle with her. When she got her boots out of the cupboard I did my usual routine of checking them for spiders and guess what? One of her boots had some dog biscuits in that must have fallen in when Dad fed us last night. I ate them all up. Mum get's really concerned that my beard may get caught in the zip when she does them up so she always pushed me away.

When she went to leave for work, she had lost something. I helped her to look even though I didn't know what she was looking for. She had lost her car keys. She was going to be late for work so she took Dad's car instead. Dad was still quite poorly so we decided to spend the day running out in the garden. Well, it didn't take long for us all to get really tired.

Mum came home and noticed I had a sore on my belly. I have licked my tummy a bit too much so Mum put some cream on it. Dad said that if I didn't stop licking it then he would put that plant pot thing on my neck. I don't want that so I stopped licking right away.

We had our usual evening in front of the tv and then all had an early night again as we are all so tired still from Dad being ill.

Friday 22nd February

I got up this morning and did my usual routine. I have now added annoying the cat to my morning antics. She usually gets up on the table and I try and play catch the cat paw. I'm not really very good at t as she has those knives on her paws and they can really hurt.

The sun was shining today so once Mum had gone to work I went out and played for most of the day. It was great to feel that lovely sun on my face again. Me and Rosie played chase a lot and I soon got very tired out.

Mum came home and I woke up and played with her. Dad is still poorly and so I kept going up to him and gave him lots of hugs. In the evening Mum and Dad watched tv and we all cosied up on the sofa until bed time.

Saturday 23rd February

Mum got up really early this morning, 4.30am to be exact. She woke me up and let me out for a wee and then I went and had a nap on the sofa. I can't believe how early we got up. After a while we woke up properly and me and Rosie thought we would have a play on the sofa, Mum took a picture of us playing and then told us to stop, we pulled a face at her when she told us to stop and Mum took another picture and then laughed a lot and said we were both silly.

Dad got up and was still coughing. He said sorry to Mum for keeping her awake all night. He can't help it but I wish he would get better. Mum went out shopping and then Aunty Bean came. We said hello and then went back to sleep as we were so tired.

In the afternoon Mum took out a blanket and put it on the decking, it was like the old days, me and Rosie got on it right away and lay in the sun. It was lovely.

I stayed out for most of the day and really loved watching the birds flying about. I can't understand how they do it. When I try to do it I jump in the air and always land again. It's not fair, I would love to be able to fly.

In the evening we all chilled out on the blanket that had been bought back in to the house and we all curled up and slept on it until bedtime.

Sunday 24th February

We got up at a better time today. I love Sundays. It's the best day of the week. We watched Hollyoaks again because I really love the music to it. The guitar bit is fab. Dad then went into the kitchen and started to cook our usual big roast. Now I am a big boy I get to have the same as the others as my belly can cope with it now.

After lunch we went out onto the blanket in the sun again and I helped Mum do some gardening. It was a bit half hearted though as I felt full and sleepy after my big lunch.

We stayed out until it started to get cold and then all came in and snuggled up on the blankets until it was time for us to all go to bed.

Monday 25th February

160

This morning I heard Mum get up at around 3.30am, she went and lay on the sofa and went to sleep. Dad must have woken her up coughing again. I think he should go to the vets really as I am starting to think he may have that kennel cough thing. Later on Mum woke up and got ready for work.

Dad came downstairs and was still coughing. I do feel sorry for him. I gave him big cuddles to see if that would help. It didn't so I went off to play with the cat for a while. Later on I assisted Dad with the housework and then went out. I like going out, it's good fun. Dad said we will be going back up to that field soon as Rosie is looking a lot better now. I can't wait. I can practise my running like the wind thing. Mum and Dad said that I can practise more now as my muscles are starting to build. Apparently when you are a puppy you have to be careful when you run as you may hurt your bones and your legs won't grow properly. I didn't know that.

When Mum came home, Dad went out for a while, I was really naughty with Mum. I emptied a plant pot of earth over the garden and then when Mum told me off I barked at her. She ended up really telling me off. Apparently I need to learn my manners. Well, I behaved well for the rest of the day. I didn't like being told off by Mum.

I was happy to get to bed tonight as being woken up again so early tired me out. I went into my crate and snuggled down and slept really well.

Tuesday 26th February

I woke up and went out for my morning wee. I could see it was going to be a lovely and warm day. I came back in and had a cuddle with Mum and then checked her boots to make sure there was nothing in them before she put them on. She gets really worried when I do that though as she said she could trap my beard in her zip.

When Mum had gone to work, Dad opened the back door and we all went out into the garden and I played with Rosie and Maizie until I was worn out. All this running is making my muscles grow really big now. I feel really strong and am able to run really fast now.

Mum came home and I got really excited, she was late today as she had to go to hospital for more scans. I really don't know what is going on as she doesn't seem poorly.

In the evening I played with the cat for a while and then snuggled up on the sofa until bed time.

Wednesday 27th February

I got up this morning and the weather was nice again. I had my usual routine of cuddles with Mum and then checking her boots for things that shouldn't be in there. When Dad got up I had my breakfast and then got up onto Dad's lap for my daily shoulder rub.

We all went out and had some fun and then played with our toys in the afternoon. I managed to help Dad with the housework, he still looks quite poorly and I do worry about him quite a lot. But he isn't coughing as much now. I still think it would be a good idea for him to have the stuff up his nose like we do because that is medicine to make sure we don't catch any coughs.

Mum was late home again today but seemed very happy. She had been to see the doctor at the hospital and apparently is able to help fix Dad. That sounds brilliant.

I always get really excited when Mum comes home and jump up at her. She tries hard to stop me but I love it when she comes home. I don't mean to hurt her when I jump up but I suppose I am very tall now. I must try harder to be a good boy.

We had our usual cuddles in the evening and then all happily went to bed.

Thursday 28th February

I got up this morning and the weather was rubbish. All the ground was wet and I ran back inside after my morning wee. I had a cuddle with Mum and then checked her boots again. I still hope to find another dog biscuit in them like I did last week.

162

Mum went to work and Dad went out to do the shopping, he didn't do a very good job as there were no special treats for us. I was not amused. I also didn't want to go out today, I hate the rain as much as Rosie does. I would rather play indoors and keep my feet dry.

Mum came home today at her proper time, I was so excited to see her and jumped all over her. She kept telling me off and I took no notice until she got the wooden spoon out of the draw and started to chase me around the dining room table with it. It was really funny. She waves it at me but I know she won't ever hit me with it so all is good.

I went outside when she wasn't looking and started to play with my boy bits again. Mum always tells me off when I do that and said that the vet told her I had to stop doing it. Mum keeps saying I will lose my balls soon. We have lots of balls in the house so I hope she doesn't take them all away as they are my favourite toys.

In the evening I chilled out on the sofa with Mum and Rosie until it was time for bed.

Friday 1st March

I got up this morning and went out for my usual morning wander around the garden. I came back in, had a cuddle with Mum and then checked her boots to make sure there were no hidden things in them. I decided today that I would be a good boy. After Mum went to work I went and had my breakfast and then assisted Dad with the chores. I still haven't managed to kill the hoover yet but I will get it in the end.

The rest of the day was the usual run of the mill day and nothing out of the ordinary occurred really, well, not until Mum came home anyway. She came back with the biggest bag of tripe sticks I had ever seen. She went into the kitchen and opened the bag and gave us one each. I love tripe sticks, they are very tasty.

I played with Mum and the other two dogs until tea time and then I had my tea. We then were given a venison treat each, I also thought they were very tasty too. I like trying out new food, I haven't really tasted anything yet that I don't like.

In the evening we all snuggled up in the front room and Mum and Dad watched tv. We got a bit of pizza crust and then all went off to bed.

Saturday 2nd March

I woke Mum up this morning as it was daylight and she was still in bed. Mum was not amused. Apparently, the mornings are getting lighter earlier now and I need to understand this or Mum will be awake very early at weekends soon.

Once she was up and properly awake she gave us our breakfast, then she started to make something out of cardboard and cloth. I was very interested in what she was doing so I sat and watched her all morning, so did Maizie. After she had finished I could see it was a top hat. Mum says there is a picture of a dog that looks like me wearing a hat like that. Then I worked out what Mum was up to. She tried to get me to put the hat on, that was a big no from me. I like my head just as it is thank you.

Mum put the hat on the radiator to dry out properly and I hoped she would just forget about it.

It was a horrid and rainy day today so I didn't want to go out. Every time I get wet, my fur just gets more frizzy. I don't like that very much. In the evening Mum and Dad watched a movie and me and Rosie cuddled up until it was time for bed.

Sunday 3rd March

I woke Mum up this morning as it was light again. I don't understand why she stays in bed when its daylight. She said because it was Sunday and 7am and wanted a lay in. Oh well. After she got up she went out and came back with croissants. We were allowed a small piece each. It was very yummy. Then my favourite music came on, I love Hollyoaks. I love the guitar bit, it makes my ears go funny.

164

Dad cooked the usual Sunday dinner but today we got beef. I am now nearly 10 months old so I had a proper roast like the other dogs. It is so tasty. I love Sundays.

In the afternoon we all got on the sofa and went to sleep. It was raining again so I didn't want to go out. I felt too full and fat anyway.

Later on I managed to get near that hat, so I stole the feather mum had made for it and ate it. She looked at me and just shook her head. I don't think she was overly impressed. She forgets how tall I am and that I can reach anything.

In the evening Mum watched a programme about big woolly mammoths and there was a wold head on it. I didn't really like that. I didn't understand why it was only a head. It was very weird. I decided to take myself off to bed.

Monday 4th March

I got up this morning and went out for a rainy, wet wee. I came back in and got up on the sofa with Mum, we had a bit of a cuddle and then I decided to play a new game. It's called lets try and push Mum off the sofa. I stuck my feet into Mum's back and pushed as hard as I could. It worked, she slid over to the edge of the sofa. I thought it was funny but she didn't. When she got her boots out I checked them over again and as she put them on and did up the zip she told me again to mind my beard.

I had the usual day with Dad again today, went out, got fed and tried to help with killing the hoover again.

When Mum came home I followed her right out to the kitchen and she gave me a tripe stick. I sort of get why she is doing that now as if I am polite and don't jump up at her I get a tripe stick. If I jump up she gets out the wooden spoon and shows it to me.

The evening was quiet and we all snuggled down on the sofa together until it was time for bed.

Tuesday 5th March

When I got up this morning the sky was blue and it looked like it was going to be a sunny day. I came back in and played the push Mum off the sofa game again. She did laugh today so I think she doesn't mind me wanting to play at that time in the morning. I inspected her boots again and then she went off to work.

The weather didn't stay nice for long. Just after Mum left it started to rain and then it was like that pretty much all day. No way was I going out in that. I have even learnt to hold my wee in for as long as Rosie can. She hates going out in the rain too and I am in full agreement with her. She wont even go out for a walk in the rain and to be fair, I don't want to get any frizzier either.

We amused ourselves by playing with our toys and helping Dad with the housework. When Mum came home I was the best I had ever been, I walked into the kitchen with her and then got my tripe stick. I didn't jump up at her once. I was very good and she was very pleased.

I am now slowly learning that if I do good things I get loads of rewards, I especially like having my ears and back rubbed. That feels wonderful. In the evening I snuggled down with Mum and Rosie on the sofa and got more rubs and cuddles. I really liked it. Rosie went to bed really early tonight so I also went to bed. Mum and Dad then decided they would go to bed early too.

Wednesday 6th March

I woke up this morning and went out for my wee. The weather was rubbish today and it was raining so I was as quick as I could be. I came back in and had cuddles and a bit of a play with Mum. I tried to push her off the sofa again this morning but she told me off so instead I asked to have my belly rubbed. I really like that and Mum always ends up smiling when she rubs my belly.

After Mum went to work I had the usual day, went out, came home, had some food and then had a sleep until Mum came home. When she got home I knew I had to be good if I wanted one of those yummy tripe sticks so I didn't jump up at all. I was very good and took my stick into my crate to eat. They smell really lovely, although it must be only us dogs that think that as Mum keeps them sealed up in the bag and then puts them in a plastic box.

After I ate my stick I practiced my zoomies again, Mum, Rosie and Maizie can all hear me coming and I love the way everyone jumps out of my way. I soon got bored of that so I had another play with the cat. Mum gets so worried when I play with the cat as she looks so tiny compared to me, but she chases me too and Mum seems to forget that.

In the evening we all chilled out in front of the tv, but Mum and Dad were both really tired so we all had a very early night tonight. I didn't mind that though as my crate is so warm and cozy.

Thursday 7th March

This morning it was dry. I went out in the garden and spent quite a while sniffing around. I find strange smells in the mornings when it's dry and I think cats come into the garden when they know I am in bed. I don't really like this because I don't mind the cat I live with but am not happy thinking other, strange ones are visiting.

Mum called me back in so I went and had some cuddles with her before she went to work. This week she has been at work longer than usual, but she said it won't be for long and then she will be able to stay home with me a bit more often. She said she has someone working with her now who is going to take over. Wow, I didn't realise Mum was the boss. I must listen to her more often I think.

I had another usual run of the mill day with nothing really to report. I still haven't managed to kill the hoover but I'm sure one day I will.

When Mum came home I was good again and she gave us another tripe stick. They were rubbish today as they were so small. We all protested so she gave us another one each to make up for it.

In the evening we all got on the sofa and cuddled up together, it was quite chilly tonight, Dad went to bed really early so we stayed up to keep Mum company until she went to bed.

Friday 8th March

This morning was really cold so when I went out for my wee I thought I would warm myself up by running up and down on the decking. Mum came out and told me off. Apparently it is rude to do that at 6am as I am to noisy. I went back in and decided to play with the cat, yet again I got told off for making too much noise. I came up with a plan. Mum went in the bathroom to get ready for work so I picked up one of Dad's slippers and took it into my crate.

When Mum got out of the bathroom so came looking for me and wondered why I was so quiet. She was really not happy when she saw I had eaten a big hole in the bottom of Dad's slipper. She took it off me and said Dad would be cross.

The rest of the day was pretty much like normal, went out, played, ate and slept until Mum came home. When Mum came back she was earlier like normal. I was very happy to see her and jumped all over her again. She was not amused.

In the evening we all chilled out in front of the tv until bedtime.

Saturday 9th March

I got up this morning and it was a bit cold and windy. I found Dad's slipper again and played with that for a while. After breakfast Parlsa arrived. She bought a big bag with her. It was fab, she made us some new toys, she is clever, she gets a ball off wool and a little stick and makes all sorts of toys, today we got a leek, a turnip and a carrot. That kept us happy for ages.

Later on in the afternoon someone came to the door and gave Mum a big box. When she opened it we were all really happy, it was a massive

168

bucket and it was full of tripe sticks. They were much better than the ones we usually have as they were so big.

Parlsa went home around tea time, we had our tea and then we basically slept for the rest of the day because we were worn out with all the playing and excitement.

We all chilled out in front of the tv tonight and Rosie went to bed really early, it was only 8.30 so I stole her space on the sofa and cuddled up with Mum until bedtime.

Sunday 10th March

I got up this morning and the weather was rubbish. I know that today is the best day of the week though so I can put up with rubbish weather on a Sunday. I watched Hollyoaks again like I do every week, I so love the music they play on it. After Hollyoaks finished I went and watched Dad get everything ready for dinner. I often catch a piece of carrot or something if it falls on the floor.

Dinner was fab, it was roast chicken. I had the works, all the veg, potatoes and chicken. It was lovely. I then went to make sure Rosie and Maizie hadn't left any behind in their dishes. After dinner there was a knock on the door. It was Jamie and Dylan. I was so excited. I hadn't seen Dylan since I was a puppy. He was very surprised to see how big I am now. I managed to wash his face and had a play with him while Mum, Dad and Jamie talked a lot.

After they went I was tired again so I got up on the sofa with Mum and Rosie and watched a film with them. Dad was laughing a lot at the film, it had ladies in it that were fighting ghost things. Very strange if you ask me.

In the evening, we all snuggled down in the front room and then all had an early night. Rosie had gone to bed again at 8.30.

Monday 11th March

I got up this morning and went out for my usual wee. The door I use to go outside seems to be getting quite small now, I have to squeeze myself through it. I really hope it doesn't shrink anymore or I will be in trouble. When I came in I found Dad's slipper again so I decided to have another chew on it. Dad says he is going to throw them away. I think he should just let me have them. Everyone knows that dogs like slippers.

It was a rough old day today outside so we all protested that we didn't want to go out today so instead I helped Dad with the housework and then had a nice afternoon nap. I could see the bucket of tripe sticks on the table and tried several times to get Dad to give me one but he wouldn't.

Mum came home and the first thing she did was give us all a tripe stick. I was very pleased and took it off to my bed. Once I had finished chewing I went over and had a play with Mum, she asked me to calm down after a while as Rosie was sat on her lap and looked a bit annoyed with me. I think she worries that I may hurt her by accident. I wouldn't do that though as love Rosie so much. She is my best friend.

In the evening we all hung out in the front room and I played with my back leg for a while until I decided I was tired and wanted to go to bed. I am still really wishing that the nice warm and sunny weather will come back. I hope that wasn't just a thing that happens when you are a puppy. I don't want it to rain forever.

Tuesday 12th March

I woke up this morning and Mum wouldn't let me out until she had checked the fence. It was so windy last night and I was up almost all night listening to it. I really don't like all this horrid weather. Mum eventually let me out and then after my wee I came back in and had a cuddle with Mum.

Yet again we all refused to go out at all apart from when we needed a wee as it was raining so hard all day. We had fun helping Dad with the housework and then we played with all our toys that Parsla had made. It was a pretty boring day to be fair.

Mum came home at her usual time and gave us all a tripe stick. She still moans about the smell. I think it's really funny how smells we like humans think smell horrible. Although Mum does not eat any sort of meat by the look of it.

In the evening we played a bit and then I got really cuddly with Mum. She said she much prefers to have cuddles than to get bitten. Mum and Dad watched tv until bedtime and then we all went to bed and hoped that the wind would calm down so we could all get some sleep.

Wednesday 13ᵗʰ March

I got up this morning and it was raining yet again. I am fed up with this weather now. I just want to be out running around in fields and in the garden but I really don't want to get wet. I came back in and cuddled up with Mum, but I soon got bored of that so I went and saw if Rosie wanted to play with me. Rosie got up and we started to play but Mum said it was far too early. I really wanted to play this morning so I barked at Mum. She told me to be quiet as Dad was still sleeping. Then Rosie joined in with me. Mum then really got cross so we just lay on the sofa together grumbling quietly together.

After Mum went to work, Dad gave us our breakfast and then did the housework. It was still blowing a gale outside and we didn't want to go out at all. I stayed in and played with Rosie and Maizie and played with my toys.

Mum came home and shouted hello as she came in, it was really funny as Rosie said hello back. Apparently she used to do it all the time but stopped when Zak died. She has said hello a few times but not often, I wonder if she will do it every day now, if she does I may be able to learn how to do it too. That would be really good fun. Mum gave us our hide chews and we went into our beds to eat them.

In the evening I had a play with Mum and then settled down on the sofa and cuddled up with Mum and Rosie until it was time for bed. I really hope tonight is quieter as I need a decent night's sleep with no sound of wind.

171

Thursday 14th March

I woke up this morning and yet again it was a horrid day, it was really windy and raining a lot. I went out and had a very quick wee and then went and had a cuddle with Mum. I have totally got it sussed now that if I hit Mum with my paw then she will stroke me. I like this, Mum says I hit a bit hard though.

So I had a usual day again today, I played a bit and then attacked the hoover. It is a very strong thing as I still haven't managed to hurt it. Dad noticed I had a sore paw today. He was most concerned and when Mum got home he asked her to look at it. Mum said it was just a small scratch but that we would keep an eye on it as there is a nasty illness which makes dogs poorly, it's called Alabama Rot. That sounds nasty. I don't want that thank you.

In the evening we chilled out in front of the tv and all in all it was a quiet day. I went to bed and listened to the wind blowing.

Friday 15th March

I got up this morning and no surprise, it was raining. I am so fed up with the rain now. I want it to be warm and sunny like it used to be.

I had a nice long cuddle with Mum until she went to work and then Dad gave us our breakfast. I helped Dad with his daily chores and had a nap in the crate in the afternoon while Dad went out and got us more food.

In the afternoon it stopped raining so I went out and had a good mooch around the garden to see if there was anything new out there. I had a good run about with Rosie until it started to rain again and then we all came back inside. I hate getting wet.

The evening was the usual Friday night, Mum had some wine and we got some pizza. Life is pretty good really, apart from the weather of course.

We went to bed pretty early tonight, but I didn't mind that at all.

Saturday 16th March

I got up this morning and yes, you guessed it, it was raining. I am so fed up with the rain now. I need some sunshine. We had breakfast and then Mum and Dad did some housework. The morning was pretty boring really. I played with my toys and with Rosie and Maizie.

A bit later in the day, Dad started to clear the boot of the car, we watched him through the window. Rosie and Maizie started to get excited so I did too. Mum put some wellies on and then we all went out to the car. Rosie and Maizie jumped into the back of the car but I insisted on being picked up. I really don't like getting in the car by myself so I like to be helped in. I think Mum and Dad find this hard as they say I am very heavy.

We drove for about 10 minutes and then they opened the boot. We were back in that field again. Rosie and Maizie had things over their faces, I think it's so they can't nip each other when we are running. There was a fence and on the other side was some dogs with their Mum. We all ran up to the fence and then ran away as fast as we could around the field. The other dogs just watched us. I think they were wishing they could run as fast as we can. We had such a good time and I even managed to forget that it was raining.

Even though I am getting to be big now, I still couldn't keep up with Rosie. I did try really hard though and I am sure as time goes on I will beat her.

We all got back in the car and came home after our run. We were all so tired that we had a drink of water and slept all afternoon. My feet ached a bit from all that running but I really love that field. I cant wait to go back again soon.

We all went to bed early tonight and left Mum and Dad to watch tv on their own.

Sunday 17th March

I had a lay in this morning and when I got up eventually I saw it wasn't raining. I went out and had a wee and a good sniff around. I came back in and had a cuddle with Mum. When Dad got up I thought we were going to

173

watch Hollyoaks but we didn't. Mum and Dad started to tidy up. Mum did the hoovering today and I was not happy with this. I don't want the hoover to hurt my Mum. I attacked it more than I do with Dad as I needed to protect her. Mum thought it was quite funny.

Grandad turned up just before lunch and then Granny came in from next door. They had come for lunch. I was worried that there wouldn't be enough left over for us, and then I saw the big chicken come out of the oven. Yummy, I was going to get a big chicken dinner.

After they had all eaten their dinner, Mum tidied up the kitchen and gave us our dinner. It was so lovely and I felt very full and fat after eating that. We all had a snooze after Granny and Grandad had gone home.

Mum took some new shoes out of the cupboard later and put them on to go outside. I remembered them, they are the shoes she wore when the weather was lovely when I was a puppy. I got quite excited about this. I think maybe the sun will start to come back soon.

In the evening Mum and Dad were watching the tv, I managed to sneak over and take one of Mum's shoes. As I chewed it, it sounded just like my crock used to sound when I chewed that. Mum suddenly realised I was eating her shoe and came and took it off me She ruins all my fun.

We all went to be quite tired today, it was a very busy day and I know that Mum has to get up early for work tomorrow so we all went to bed and fell asleep right away.

Monday 18th March

I got up early with Mum this morning and went out to check over the garden and have a wee. I came back in and had a big cuddle with Mum. I seem to be squashing her these days, she isn't as big to me as she used to be. I now take up her whole lap and I can hear her groaning that I am too heavy.

After Mum had gone to work Dad did the usual chores and I assisted like normal with trying to protect him from the hoover. It was a dull and rainy day again and not very warm so I amused myself in the house for most of the day until Mum came home.

When Mum got home I had a tripe stick and then barked at her to play with me. She will learn one day that I don't like to take no for an answer. For the rest of the evening we chilled out in front of the tv until it was time for bed.

Tuesday 19th March

I got up this morning and it wasn't raining for a change. I went out, had a quick wee and then came back to annoy my Mum. I like getting behind her on the sofa and I use my feet to try and push her off, I can nearly do it now. Mum went off to work as usual and then I helped Dad with his chores.

Around lunchtime I was really surprised as Mum came home. She put on trousers again, that only means one thing to me, we were going to the field. I was so excited. I really love it there. I can run really fast and it's just great. We arrived at the field and when Dad opened the boot we all jumped out and ran the full length of the field. On the way back to Mum and Dad we nearly ran into a drinking trough, Rosie literally just managed to jump over it in time.

We walked around the field for ages and at one point Rosie ran into Mum, she made her leg very sore and there was a big lump on Mum's shin. We loved running around and it was lovely and sunny today so we all got really warm.

When it was time to come home I made Mum lift me into the boot again. I think it's funny because I could hop into it easily but I like it better that Mum has to pick me up. We got home and then we all fell asleep until tea time as we were so tired.

In the evening we all got on the sofa and dozed until bedtime and then I went to bed dreaming about my next trip to the big field. Life is getting really exciting now with being able to finally run as much as I want without hurting my puppy legs and the weather seems to be getting better.

175

Wednesday 20th March

I got up this morning and went outside for a wee and a sniff about before I went in to annoy Mum. I love trying to push her off the sofa with my feet and now I am so big and strong it is quite easy to do. I annoyed Mum today right up until she left for work.

Once Mum had gone I had my usual day of helping Dad with the housework and hoovering and then I went out. When I got back I played with Maizie and Rosie and once they got bored I had a look around to see what I could do next. I noticed that on top of my crate there are some plants growing. They smell just like the beans that Mum grew last year. I really hope it is beans as last year I managed to pick some to eat and this year I am a lot taller so I will be able to reach more.

Dad popped out and gave us all a stuffed bone each, they were so tasty and we didn't even bother saying hello to Mum when she got home. She got to have a glass of wine in peace tonight, I suppose she does deserve it. I didn't even notice that Mum had bought home some new slippers

After tea, Dad felt poorly again so he got a blanket and went to sleep in this chair. I worry about Dad as he is poorly a lot and I don't like it at all. Mum said that he will be better one day but to get better we will all have to go to kennels while Mum and Dad go to hospital. I'm not sure what kennels is yet.

In the evening we were all quiet so as not to disturb Dad. We got up on the sofa and cuddled up with Mum until it was time to go to bed. I got in my crate and slept really well.

Thursday 21st March

I got up this morning and went out for my usual wee. I had a good sniff about and then came back in to cuddle on the sofa and try and push Mum off it. Once Mum had gone to work I helped Dad with the housework. We were supposed to be going to that lovely field again today but at the last minute Mum had to cancel as she had to stay on at work. I wish Mum wasn't the boss as she doesn't really get much time off. She hasn't had a holiday since the week they went up to get me in the summer.

When Mum got home she gave us a chew each and then we had a play and a cuddle. Today was pretty much a usual day with nothing much really to report. It was a good day but nothing really to write about so I just took myself off to bed.

Friday 22nd March

I got up and went for a wee, it was dry outside so I stayed out for quite a while and watched all the big black crows flying around, I wish I could jump up and catch them but they fly too high for me to reach. When I came back in Mum was looking a bit worried. There were noises coming from the fireplace. I could hear it too. It sounded like things were falling down the chimney. I thought only Father Christmas did that.

Dad got up and he could hear it too. He said he would just shout if he heard a big noise to get all us dogs out of the way.

Mum went to work so I decided to take myself off out to the garden again and try and catch those crows. I just got really tired trying and never did catch any. So I decided that it would be better if I played with the other dogs instead.

When Mum came home she had bought us new chews as we had eaten all the tripe sticks, these were called dentastix, I wasn't so keen on them. I like my tripe sticks. Mum looked pretty tired when she got home and so she had a glass of wine and I curled up on the sofa with her to keep her warm and cozy. We watched tv in the evening and then all went to bed.

Saturday 23rd March

I woke up this morning and the sun was shining, I thought I had better wake Mum up too so I started to quietly bark to wake her up. She came down and asked me to shut up. Apparently it was 6.30am and Mum doesn't go to work today. I went back to sleep for a bit and then woke up and was a bit bored so I decided to wake Mum up again. She came down

177

and let me out for a wee and made herself a cup of coffee and then got ready to go out.

Mum went out quite early as Dad had only just got up. She wasn't gone all day though and when she came home she had Aunty Bean with her. I got really excited to see her. Mum and Dad kept telling me off for jumping all over her.

After Aunty Bean left Mum went out into the garden so I went with her. She was looking around at what to do to make it all look better and how to fix the bits of the garden that I have wrecked.

We stayed out for quite a while and then we had another visitor. I had not met Luke before, he called me a giant. He was very nice and I think I made friends with him quite quickly.

After Luke left, we had tea and then settled down to watch movies on the tv. We were all really tired from entertaining our guests today so we all fell asleep on the sofa until bed time.

Sunday 24th March

I woke up early today again and tried to wake Mum up. She came down and told me to shut up and went back to bed for a bit. She didn't stay there long as she was now awake.

Dad got up not long after and we all watched Hollyoaks again, I love the music to that so much and also know it's the day of the roast. After Hollyoaks was finished Dad didn't go and cook roast, we were all really worried as we always have roast on Sunday.

Grandad turned up again, I felt like telling him that it was a waste of time as Dad hadn't cooked anything. Then they all got up and went out leaving us roastless. I was seriously not amused by this.

In the end they came back in and Mum had our dishes and they were full of roast dinner, Granny had cooked it for us. We were so happy. In the afternoon, Mum put blankets out on the decking for us to lay on as the sun was shining. She started working on the garden and also took all the fencing down from Zak's pond. She started to take the leaves out that had fallen in and I started to help. Mum looked a bit sad when she was doing the pond and told me that I now have to look after it like Zak did as it was his little pond. I will look after it well and make sure all the leaves that fall in are taken out. Mum then got out the table and chairs properly. Everything looks so much smaller than last year. I can't even fit under the chairs anymore. It's all a bit weird.

We stayed out until it got cold and then had tea. After tea, I was so tired that I slept on the front room floor all evening, right up until it was time to go to bed. I went to bed hoping that tomorrow would be just as nice as today.

Monday 25th March

I woke up at the usual time when Mum came down to get ready for work. It was really nice and sunny again and as soon as Mum got up she opened all the blinds and let in the morning sun. Mum asked me to check her boots this morning as she said that there is a mouse in the cupboard under the stairs and she was worried it may have hid in her boot. After a good sniff I reassured her that there was no mouse in her boot.

Mum went off to work and then I helped Dad do the hoovering and then went out to spend the day messing about in the garden. I played with the other dogs and then checked Zak's pond for leaves. Then I did what we all like doing best, I sunbathed.

I did that right up until I heard Mum's car, then I ran in to greet her. She got a glass of wine and came outside and sat with us all. It feel like the good old days are finally coming back.

In the evening we watched the tv and then we all went to bed, it was quite early but I was very tired.

Tuesday 26th March

Today I got up and went out for my morning wee. There was nothing to report there so I came back in for Mummy cuddles. Mum cuddled me until it was time for her to get ready for work and then when she went not the cupboard to get her coat she noticed that there was another mouse in the trap. She took it down the garden and I watched it run under the fence to the neighbours garden.

I am apparently the kind of dog that should catch mice. I can't do that, that would be mean. I don't like to hurt anything.

I helped Dad with all the housework like I usually do and still didn't manage to kill the hoover. I do try so hard though. Mum ended up coming home early and guess where we went? We went to that big field again. I love it there as I can run really fast and chase the other two dogs.

We got home and I was so very tired. I had a treat and then had a very long nap until tea time. Mind you, once I had tea I went back to sleep again. I was so tired out from all that running around.

In the evening we all settled down in front of the tv and dozed until bedtime.

Wednesday 27th March

Today was a pretty boring day really. I get up, had a wee, had a cuddle with Mum before she went to work and then spent most of the day playing with the other dogs. I chased the hoover and today I just feel like a puppy that has very little to write about. It wasn't a bad day but it wasn't anything really to write home about.

I settled down on the sofa in the evening with Mum and Rosie and pretty much stayed there until it was time to go to bed.

Thursday 28th March

Today I got up and went out for a wee, there were no mice today so I came back in and had a cuddle with Mum. I helped Dad with the housework as per usual and then amused myself by playing with Rosie and Maize. The cat didn't seem very well today. Mum told me that she is really old and that she can have days like that so I left her alone today.

Mum said she is nearly 15. I think that is pretty old as Maizie looks old and she is only 10.

In the afternoon, Mum came home and played with me a lot. It was great fun, although she still complains about all her bruises. I don't bite hard so I don't get what she is moaning about.

We all chilled out in the evening and watched tv until it was time for bed.

Friday 29th March

Today I got up, went for a wee and then came back in for a Mummy cuddle. I was surprised as she didn't get ready for work. It was all a bit odd. She got dressed and then we all got in the car and went to the field again. I love it there. I run like the wind. Mum and Dad split up and walked in opposite directions and we didn't know what to do so we ran between them both. I was so tired after a while. It was mad running so much. Even Maizie was running more than usual, but that's because she had been to the vet and had a manicure according to Mum.

In the afternoon, we were so tired that we were quite happy to go in our beds and sleep while Mum and Dad went out. They weren't gone for too long and when they came back they ordered Chinese and we got prawn crackers. I love them. They are so tasty.

Mum and Dad watched tv for the rest of the evening and we all dozed on the sofa until it was time to go to bed.

Saturday 30th March

Today we all got up later. It was nice to see a sunny day too. Mum made herself a cup of coffee and then we had a nice cuddle on the sofa. I stayed on the sofa for a while and then Mum got up and went out for a while. When Mum came back her hair looked really nice, she had been up and had it done by a lady who makes Mum's hair look really nice.

When Mum got back, Mum and Dad emptied out everything in the cupboard under the stairs so they could look to see if there were any more mice. They emptied everything out. I had to help and sniffed all the shoes to make sure that there was no mice in any of them.

We found no mice at all so Mum and Dad put everything away again. We then had tea and after tea Jamie and Parlsa came over. It was good fun and I managed o get some food out of everyone. They stayed really late and by the time they went it was around 3.30 in the morning. I was so very tired and glad to get to bed.

Sunday 31st March

Today I got up later again. Mum said it was even later as the time had moved forward an hour. I don't understand why but it was ok. Mum looked a bit poorly and said it was because she drank too much wine. She didn't look very well.

It was a nice day again so I went out to play in the garden and then I heard a knock at the door. It was Grandad. He had come for lunch again. Granny also turned up. I went into my crate and pulled faces at them to make them laugh. I put my top lip on one of the wires and then stick my tongue out so all my teeth are showing. It really does make everyone laugh.

After everyone had gone, we all got a roast chicken dinner, I love Sundays. After lunch we watched Hollyoaks. I still really love the music. We all snuggled down for the rest of the afternoon and evening and watched movies.

Rosie went to bed at 8pm and I cuddled up with Mum until she went to bed.

Monday 1st April

I woke up this morning and Mum didn't go to work. She had a morning coffee and then once Dad was ready we all got in the car and went to the field again. I really do love it at the field. I chased Rosie for ages and then Maizie also joined in. Her feet must be feeling so much better now.

I do find it hard being in the boot though as we seem to be very squashed now. Mum and Dad say it's because I am so big now and Dad says he needs a bigger car.

When we got back from the field, we all went out and sunbathed in the garden on our blankets. It was lovely to feel the sun warming us up and we stayed out there until it got chilly.

In the evening we all snuggled down in front of the tv and stayed there until bedtime when we all happily took ourselves off to bed.

Tuesday 2nd April

I got up later again today as Mum wasn't going to work again. I love having her home. It's great. We had a pretty usual day again today, we sunned ourselves in the garden and played a lot. Mum did some gardening and then cleaned out the fish filter on the pond, or as I like to call it, the fish pooh bucket. Mum gets really stressed cleaning that out and says there are little worm things that will suck your blood if they get on you. Well, I had to go and have a look. I couldn't see anything.

In the evening we all had a really early night, I was starting to sense that something was going to be happening soon but I couldn't work out what. I went off to bed wondering.

Wednesday 3rd April

I got up this morning and had a cuddle with Mum. Dad got up and then they got ready to go out. Rosie and Maizie started to get a bit excited so I thought we must be going to the field. We all got in the car and off we went. It was a longer car ride than usual and that got alarm bells ringing for me.

When the car stopped and we got out, Maizie and Rosie ran into a building where there was a nice girl. Mum handed her our vet books and a

183

bag of food and treats and then we were taken away from Mum and Dad. I was put into a room with Rosie, It looked just like the room I was born in. Oh my God, Mum and Dad don't want us anymore, I thought they had given us away to a shelter. I then heard the car go away. Oh no, this wasn't good.

After Mum and Dad had gone, the girl took us all out to a field and we played. I forgot for a while that we had been abandoned so I got to have a good play and tire myself out.

In the evening the girls came and gave us tea but I didn't want mine. I just felt really sad. I went to bed worrying a fair bit

Thursday 4th April

I got up early this morning as I couldn't sleep. I missed mum and Dad so much. How could they do this to me?? I thought they loved me. Rosie didn't seem very fussed that we had been dumped. I didn't understand how she could be so calm about it all.

The girls gave us breakfast and then let us out to play again. I do like the big field but going for a walk without Mum and Dad isn't as nice.

The girls were a bit concerned that I still wasn't hungry and played with me a lot to try and cheer me up. They also tried to give me more tea again. I decided I didn't want it so I just played with my bone toy that Mum had sent up with me. I would rather have Teddy with me at the moment though. I can't understand why they didn't send Teddy with me if they were sending us to a new place to live.

I went to bed again feeling that I must have been a bad puppy in some way for Mum and Dad to not want me anymore. I curled up with Rosie and went to sleep.

Friday 5th April

I got up this morning and gave Rosie a cuddle. I was getting used to being in this kennel now but I would still rather be at home. The kennel girls came and got us and offered us breakfast and then started to brush us. They put this stuff in my fur that made me smell like flowers. I don't really like being brushed but I put up with it.

I could hear a car in the distance and as it got closer I recognised the sound of it. It was Dad's car. I got so excited. The girls put us all on our leads and packed our dishes and toys away. We went back out into the main area and Mum and Dad were stood there. I was so happy to see them. The girls told Mum and Dad that I had been very good, but hadn't eaten much. Well, what did they expect?

We all got in the car and went home. I was so glad to get home and even the cat came in to say hello. I was a bit upset with Mum and Dad so after while I decided to ignore them for the rest of the day. I turned my back on the pair of them and then went to sleep until bedtime. I was so happy to finally be back in my own bed.

Saturday 6ᵗʰ April

I got up this morning and was so happy to be back at home. I slept really well. I decided I would stop punishing Mum and Dad now so I gave them both big cuddles when they got up. Mum was really busy today and washed all our bedding. She had the washing line full all day, it was so lovely and sunny today and I was still so very tired so I went and slept out on the blankets in the sun.

I slept again for most of the day and in the evening Mum and Dad ordered some pizza, they gave us some and then I truly forgave them for sending me away for a few days. But I just hope they don't do it again. I like being in my house and fully intend on staying here forever.

I went to bed really early again and I think tomorrow is Sunday so I wanted to be ready for my Sunday roast.

Sunday 7ᵗʰ April

I got up this morning and yippee, it's roast day. Mum and Dad had a morning coffee and then they got ready to go out. Luckily, they left us at home. When they got back, Dad started to cook lunch, but he didn't put

185

my Hollyoaks for me. Instead I went into the kitchen and watched him cook lunch. I even got some raw cauliflower and carrots.

After Mum and Dad had their lunch Mum did ours, the cat just had chicken and we had a proper roast each. It was very yummy. Then Mum and Dad put Hollyoaks on. I was still really tired though so I slept through most of it. I couldn't really be bothered still to do very much so I had a little play with Maizie and Rosie and then at around 8pm Rosie went to bed.

Mum didn't stay up very late so I guessed that Mum will be going back to work tomorrow. I was happy to go back to bed tonight. There is nothing better than your own bed in your own house!

Monday 8th April

I got up with Mum this morning. I didn't really want to get up as I was cozy in my lovely bed. I eventually got up and had cuddles with Mum on the sofa until it was time for her to go to work. O am very glad life has got back to normal again now and I don't think Mum and Dad should ever leave me again.

After Mum went to work, Dad started to take everything out of the front room, I'm not sure why but at least our sofas are still there. It was a usual day again today, went out, came back and played for a bit.

When Mum got home we all went out into the garden and sat in the sun for a bit until it was time for tea. We all had our tea and then we all cuddled up in the front room and watched tv until bedtime. I was glad again to get to bed tonight.

Tuesday 9th April

Today I got up and had a cuddle with Mum and then went for a run around the garden. Mum came out and told me off and said I was being too noisy. I came back in and had cuddles with Mum and then she went to work again. It was a lovely sunny day so we all decided to spend the day out in the garden as Dad was busy moving things around the house again and then he got this big bit of plastic stuff and made doors and windows out of it in the front room.

Mum also looked surprised when she got in and decided to sit outside for a bit too. We sat outside for quite a while and it was really nice in the sun. After tea we all snuggled up on the sofa but I kept looking around and wondering why Dad had put up all the plastic and wondered where all the stuff had gone from the mantle piece and table. I went to bed thinking and wondering what has going to happen as I got the feeling something is amiss.

Wednesday 10th April

I got up this morning and Mum wasn't going to work. I had cuddles with her on the sofa and then she got dressed and got us all in the car. I had the whole boot to myself which was much better and Rosie and Maizie sat on the back seat which now has a cover on it. We arrived at the field and had a really good run about. It was good fun but Dad wasn't with us.

Once we got really tired, Mum took us home. Dad was putting this big machine thing together, it didn't look like a hoover though. Suddenly I heard a really loud noise from behind the plastic and I could see dust coming through the gaps in the plastic. It was so loud that I decided to go outside.

After a while Dad started to bring big bags of stuff out and helped Mum put them in the car. It turns out they are taking down a fireplace. Mum explained that we will even be getting a new sofa.

In the evening we all had to sit in the dining room. It isn't very big and we were all a bit annoyed so we all go in our beds. There was a knock on the door and Chinese food arrived. I was really happy because Mum gave us all prawn crackers. They are so yummy and we really enjoyed them.

We had a really early night tonight as everyone was fed up with the mess.

Thursday 11th April

When Mum got up today I didn't want to. I didn't like all the mess everywhere and because Mum was sitting at the table I couldn't sit on her lap for a cuddle. I hated all the chaos and just wanted my sofa back.

Mum went to work and Dad went in behind the plastic sheet again. Once again we had to listen to all that noise so we all decided to go and sit in the sun. After a while, the noise stopped and then Dad got the hoover out and took it behind the plastic. He was there for ages.

Dad bought the hoover back out and a load of blankets and then took down the plastic sheet. I rushed in and got straight up on the sofa and Rosie was right behind me. We were very happy to get it back.

Mum came home and cheered and we all got up on the sofa. The big stone fireplace was gone and Mum seemed very happy about this. I do think they are doing to do more stuff to this room though as it looks a bit untidy where the fire was. I guess we will have to wait and see what happens next.

Tonight me and Rosie got on the sofa with Mum and stayed there all evening. It was so nice to all be able to sit together again. We stayed on the sofa until it was time to go to bed. I slept much better tonight though.

Friday 12th April

I woke up this morning and went out for my usual morning wee. When I came back in Rosie was trying to get to the sack of food so Mum gave us breakfast really early. Just lately we have been pretty hungry first thing, but I think that's because it now gets light so early.

After Mum went to work, Dad didn't really do as much housework as the house is pretty messy at the moment with all the work going on. It wasn't a bad day so we all decided to go out and play for the afternoon. Of course, we watched Dad eat his lunch first in case there was some left for us like there usually is.

Mum came home and we got all excited. She gave us some biscuits as we have run out of tripe sticks at the moment. Mum says they are expensive so we can't get used to having them all the time.

In the evening we all crashed out on the sofa and watched tv for the night. All the upheaval of the week had made us all pretty tired and we were all really happy to get to bed.

Saturday 13th April

I woke up this morning and decided to wake Mum and Dad up. Dad came down and told me off and went back to bed again. Eventually Mum got up and gave us all breakfast. When we all went out for a wee I decided that it was really cold so I didn't want to go outside again. Mum wasn't happy today and she looked quite ill. She says its flowers that are making her poorly.

I went back into my crate for another nap when Mum and Dad went out. They went to look at stuff for the house apparently. I will be so glad when the house is back to normal. Although I like the way the speaker thing is on the floor now because I like putting my nose against it and listening to the sounds that come out. It also makes Mum and Dad laugh as they say I look like the HMV dog, whoever he was.

The rest of the day involved a short outing with nothing to report and then cuddles on the sofa while Mum watched a film and then in the evening Dad joined in and we all watched movies together until it was time to go to bed.

Sunday 14th April

I woke up this morning and went out for my wee, it was still really cold outside but at least it is a Sunday so I know that today is a dossing around watching Hollyoaks and then I get my big roast dinner.

We watched the tv and then Mum turned Hollyoaks off half way through as she said she had a few things to do. She went upstairs to feed the tortoises while Dad prepared lunch. Today's lunch was brilliant, it was massive and there was loads of chicken in it. It was very yummy.

After lunch we all went to sleep on the sofa as we were very full and I felt fat too. I had cuddles with Mum and went to sleep while they carried on watching Hollyoaks. This is the first week that I couldn't be bothered to react to the music anymore. Mum says she thinks I am growing up and thinks that's why I don't seem bothered by it anymore.

At around tea time, I went out for a bit but didn't enjoy it as it was a bit too cold. The cold made me hungry again so I started to hassle Dad for tea. After tea, we had cuddles again and I played with Mum on the sofa and then gave her really big cuddles. We all went to bed early tonight because Mum has to go to work tomorrow.

Monday 15th April

I got up early with Mum this morning. I could hear the birds singing while I was getting up. I like it as it reminds me of when I was little. Me and Rosie hassled Mum and got our breakfast early. Much better than waiting another hour for Dad to get up.

Once he got up Mum went to work and I helped Dad do the housework and yet again tried to kill the hoover. At some point I will either kill it or give up trying. I will have to wait and see what happens there.

It was a lovely day so we didn't go to the field as we had the whole garden to run about and play in and we played until lunch time and then came back in to see if we could get anything out of Dad when he ate his lunch. We got a bit of sandwich each so it was worth the effort.

We all went out and continued to play until Mum came home. She bought home tripe sticks again. We really like them, they are so tasty. In the evening me and Rosie had cuddles on the sofa and Mum took loads of photos of us. She said we looked so cute together. I really love Rosie and I know she loves me a lot too. Mum is always saying I healed her broken heart. I'm glad I did as she is so much fun to play with and has taught me so much so far.

We all cuddled up with Mum towards the end of the night and then we happily all went off to bed.

Tuesday 16ᵗʰ April

I got up to the sounds of the birds singing this morning. It was really nice. Mum came down and I had cuddles on the sofa until we decided to try and get an early breakfast again. We succeeded and then after we had eaten, Dad came down stairs and looked very weird. Mum looked shocked as Dad's face looked all swollen and sore. He sort of looked like Rosie did a while ago but without the blood.

Mum told Dad before she went to work that he needed to see a doctor. I got really worried. I don't want Dad to get sick, I love him way too much for anything to happen to him.

It was a lovely day again today so we all hung out in the garden, we played, we sunbathed and then played again. I really like it now it's getting warm again. I do think it's funny that everything seems so much smaller this year. Mum says it's because I have grown so much.

In the evening, Mum came home, she saw that Dad's face was better and I heard them say it must have been a spider that crawled in his mouth and bit him. Well, from now on I shall make sure every spider I see is eaten right away so it can't hurt Mum or Dad.

We all cuddled up on the sofa for the evening again tonight and I stayed there until it was time for bed. I really love my life I decided tonight again.

Wednesday 17ᵗʰ April

I woke up this morning and it was a lovely sunny day again. I went out for a wee and then came in and hassled Mum for breakfast with Rosie. After breakfast I went and had a cuddle with Mum until it was time for her to go to work. I really wish Mum could be home more as I like having her around the house and I get to do lots of things with her.

After Mum went off to work Dad carried on sorting out the front room. It all looks weird at the moment and I'm not really keen on it. I hope it goes back to normal soon. Me and the other dogs decided to go out in the garden and have a play for the afternoon. I managed to dig a few more holes and Dad didn't notice.

In the evening we all cuddled up on the sofa and stayed there until bedtime.

Thursday 18th April

I got up this morning and it was really sunny again. We had our breakfast and then I had a cuddle with Mum on the sofa until she went to work. She seemed quite excited today and said it was her last day at work for a few days. Excellent. I really hope that I am right and that Mum will be home for a few days.

Mum went to work and then Dad carried on with that room again. It is still not looking any better and I really don't like the dust in there. I took myself out to the garden again and stayed out there for most of the day. It was so hot today that we couldn't be bothered to even play really.

Mum came home and I had a play with her and then she went out and had a glass of wine in the garden. I sat on the swing with her. I love the swing, it reminds me of when I was a puppy.

In the evening we watched tv, Mum and Dad stayed up longer tonight and watched a film. I was quite tired so I went to bed and fell asleep right away.

Friday 19th April

Mum got up at the usual time today but didn't go to work. She sat drinking coffee until Dad got up and then they went out for a while. They came home with stuff for the front room again and Dad carried on sorting stuff out.

Mum went out into the garden and started to clear by the back door. She then went to the shed and got this big blue thing out. She turned on a machine and the blue thing started to grow. I remembered what it was. It

192

was a big bath. Last summer Mum and Dad sat in it a lot and I had to put my paws up on it to be able to see in, this year I can rest my chin on it.

Mum filled it up with water and then started to tidy the rest of the garden. She even started to measure the bottom bit of the garden. I wasn't sure why.

Mum and Dad cancelled our trip to the field today because it was so hot. Us dogs shouldn't go out running when it is really hot as it can make us ill or even worse. That's what everyone says anyway.

In the evening we stayed outside until it started to get dark and then we all went in and cuddled up on the sofa until bedtime. I went to bed dreaming of long summer nights like I had when I was a pup.

Saturday 20th April

I got up early with Mum again today and the weather was wonderful again. Mum and Dad went out really early and then came back with lots of stuff. There was also two big rolls of green stuff like we have at the bottom of the garden. Mum unrolled it and Rosie got right on it and lay down, Mum started to laugh so I decided to go and lay down next to Rosie. Mum told us we both had to move and let her get on with it so in the end we did. We sat and watched her put the new lawn over the horrible bit of ground that wasn't covered with anything.

When she had finished we played on the new grass and lay down under the apple tree for ages. It's lovely to have somewhere down the bottom to lay too. I then worked out I needed a wee, I didn't want to wee on the new grass so I went over to the hedge and worked out that if I lifted a leg I could aim higher. Mum ran in and told Dad what I had done. Apparently grown up boy dogs do it all the time and it's called cocking your leg. I think I must now be a big boy, although for the rest of the day I went back to peeing like I normally do.

In the evening I was so tired from being busy all day. I just slept for the whole evening until I went into my crate. I went to sleep right away. I was worn out from all the activities today.

Sunday 21st April

I had a bit of a lay in this morning as I was still a bit tired. Mum and Dad got up and watched Hollyoaks. I don't really bother with that music anymore. I must be getting grown up. We all went out in the garden for a while, it was really hot today. Then a while later, Grandad turned up. Dad hadn't cooked a roast so I didn't understand why Grandad was here.

It all became clear when everyone left the house. Granny had cooked dinner this week. When Mum and Dad came back, Mum had a massive bowl of food. Granny had cooked us a roast too.

We ate our dinner and then went outside. Mum and Dad were putting up the big tent thing that used to be in the garden when I first moved in. It took them ages to do and they both looked very red, I think that is because of the sun.

When it was all finished we all sat in the garden and I was very happy, it was all just how I remember it being when I moved in, apart from Mum doesn't cry like she did back then. She told me that I was getting to be a proper big boy now and I was really happy to hear that. I can't ever imagine living anywhere else.

We went indoors at the end of the evening and yet again, I fell asleep until bedtime as I was so worn out.

Monday 22nd April

I woke up this morning and realised that Mum was staying home again today. I was really happy about this. Mum and Dad went out really early but were not gone for long. They came home with all sorts of stuff and croissants too. Yummy, of course we all got a bit for breakfast.

After a while, Mum moved the tv and stuff away from the wall that they wrecked. They started to smear this mud mix all over the fireplace. It was mucky stuff and every time I tried to get a proper look I got told off. They spent most of the day doing this and I watched them mix the stuff in a bucket outside and then spread it all over the wall. It's all very odd if you ask me.

194

I decided after a while that I would go out and have a lay down on the swing again. I really do love being back outside, even if everything looks smaller this time compared with last year. So much has changed over the year, I grew to be twice the size of the other two dogs, I grew a bright red beard and the best bit is I found a brilliant forever home where I am very much loved. I love everybody too. It's weekends like the one I just had that make me a very happy young man.

In the evening, we all cuddled up on the sofa again and Rosie went to bed really early tonight. I stayed up so I could get lots of extra cuddles. I went to bed very tired, but very happy.

Tuesday 23rd April

I got up this morning and it was sunny again. I could hear what I thought was one of the other dogs running on the decking outside, well, it turns out it was the cat. I think she was stamping to make herself sound bigger. She came in and had breakfast with us and then we all settled down for a cuddle with Mum on the sofa until she went to work.

Dad carried on with building work in the front room again today. It all looks so very messy and every time I go near I get asked to move away. I only want to know what is going on. I decided in the end to go out and play and got the other two dogs to come with me. I went down and watched the tortoises for quite a while. I find them amusing, they are basically moving rocks. They are very strange.

Mum came home and went out into the garden to join us. It was very nice and Mum was pleased that I haven't wrecked anything in the garden. Well, it looks really nice now so I think I will just enjoy it now rather than trying to change it around. I am not very good at gardening.

We all went in for tea and then after we had cuddles on the sofa until Mum went in for a bath. Once I heard she was in it I sneaked in and stole her pants again. I took them and hid them in my crate. She found them when she had finished her bath and just laughed at me. Mum always laughs at me. But I don't mind that at all.

We all had a pretty early night tonight, all this decorating stuff is really tiring for all of us. I went to bed wondering what it will all look like when it's finished.

Wednesday 24th April

I got up early with Mum again today, she wasn't dressed for work today so I was excited knowing she was going to be home all day. Dad got up early today too, so I figured something was going on. Dad has a sore arm and hasn't been able to move it much, so Mum helped him. They mixed up lots of stuff and started to spread it on the wall where the fire used to be. They did that all day. Of course, I supervised. At one point I even managed to sit on Mum's lap when she was doing it so I could get a better look.

When she was out mixing some more stuff I decided to have a wee break. I went down to the bottom of the garden and had a sniff about until I found a good place to wee and then I lifted up my back leg and started to wee. I have worked out that using this technique that I can get a pretty good aim. Much better than squatting down. I think this is how I should wee from now on. I don't look like a girl then either.

Mum and Dad worked on the front room all day, by tea time they both looked like they were struggling to move around. I think they are quite old by the look of it. But I don't want them getting any older as I like my walks and trips to the field too much and I wouldn't want to go on my own.

Mum and Dad went to bed early tonight, and they said my eyes were red and that I should go to bed too. I couldn't have agreed more. Being a supervisor today was very tiring. I went to bed and was asleep very soon after.

Thursday 25th April

This morning when I got up, it had rained a lot in the night and the gazebo over the hot tub looked very wonky, I went to investigate, and Mum said I really needed to move out of the way. I didn't understand why though so I continued to have a sniff about. Mum got the broom thing and pushed up under the cover and suddenly loads of water came crashing down. I was back in through the dog flap as fast as my legs would take me. I hate getting wet, it makes my fur stick out when it dries.

Mum came back in and had coffee and a cuddle with me before she left for work. I love getting in behind her on the sofa and I stretch my legs out as much as I can to try and push her off the sofa. Then when I have her full attention I play bite the hand that feeds me. I pretend I am biting Mum's hand and then she hooks her fingers around my pointy teeth. I still try to suck her thumb too but with my new big teeth I can't do it properly anymore.

After Mum went to work it was a usual day really, I went out, I came back, I played and I helped Dad do the housework. I also had another sly inspection of the fireplace and got moved away from it.

It was quite a nice day today but a bit windy. Mum came home and went out into the garden and took the covers off the gazebo. I do hope this doesn't mean winter is coming back already. I do remember last year when I was still very little that the wind caught our big gazebo and it ended up on granny's house. Perhaps they just took the cover off so the same thing doesn't happen again.

In the evening we all stretched out on the sofa and had cuddles until it was time for bed. I went into my crate and fell asleep straight away again.

Friday 26th April

I got up this morning and it was getting a bit windy. I don't like the wind as I know it can cause loads of damage and noise. I remember when I was little and the gazebo ended up on top of granny's house.

I had a cuddle with Mum before she went to work and then I went out to check that everything was ok in the garden. Dad carried on with trying to sort out our messy house. I feel like I am very dusty at the moment and I don't like it. I decided to stay out for most of the day and let Dad get on with it.

When Mum came home she gave us more treats so we wouldn't jump up at her and then went out to see if the wind had caused any problems. It was all ok though so that was good. After tea Dad tidied up for the evening and we cuddled up on the sofa. It was a quiet day really but I don't mind them on occasion. I went to bed listening to the wind howling around the garden but I felt safe and warm in my crate.

Saturday 27th April

I woke up this morning and went out to see what had happened in the garden overnight as it was quite windy. There was a storm coming called Hannah, that's what it said on the news. I didn't want it to get any windier.

After Mum and Dad had their morning coffee, Luke arrived, he had come to fix up the front room wall. He bought in loads of stuff and I had to have a look through it all to make sure it was all safe. Mum told Luke to use the bathroom to mix the plaster as it was way too windy outside to do it. He worked hard all day sorting the wall out.

I went out into the garden and as I was there I noticed the tub of fish food on the garden table. No one was looking so I got it down and chewed the lid off. It was really smelly and tasted lovely. I ate the whole tub. Suddenly I heard the back door open and Luke caught me with the tub in my mouth and called Mum. I had been rumbled. Mum called me back in doors.

There were discussions all afternoon about how the fish food would affect me, I was fine, I just had a tasty snack as far as I was concerned. It was nice as it kept me full up until tea time.

After Luke went home Mum and Dad tidied up and then put the tv on. I thought I would get a prime spot on the sofa so up I hopped. But as I did my bottom made a really loud squeaking noise. Mum and Dad burst out laughing and said here comes the fish food.

I was ok though and every time I needed to fart I would do it quietly so they wouldn't laugh at me again. The wind outside however had got really bad and that night I went to bed listening to it howling again.

Sunday 28th April

This morning I got up and went for my wee, the only damage from the wind I could see was that one plant pot had tipped over, the plant was ok though so that was good.

I came back in and settled down on the sofa to watch Hollyoaks and wait for my roast dinner. Mum and Dad cooked dinner a bit later today and seemed to be cooking quite a bit. When it was nearly ready Luke came again with his fiancé Hannah, I thought it was funny because that was what the storm was called. She was nothing like the storm though. I really liked her and she was very gentle and nice to us all.

After they all finished lunch, we got ours. There was loads this week We all ate our lunch and then crashed out in our beds while Luke carried on sorting out the wall again. We pretty much slept for the rest of the day and let the humans get on with it.

After Luke and Hannah went, we all went back onto the sofa and snuggled up until it was time for bed. All this DIY is very tiring you know.

Monday 29th April

I got up with Mum this morning and went out for my usual wee, I came back in and then asked Mum for breakfast. We all got fed and then I got up to hassle Mum on the sofa before she went to work. Once she had gone, Dad started to take the wood off the bottom of the walls, just as it is starting to look better Dad makes more mess. It was a usual day for me until Mum came home.

Mum went out and put the roof back onto the gazebo as the wind had stopped. I tried to help but even though I am tall, I am not tall enough to help. After Mum had done that she got a big bag, when she opened it, it was full of earth. Yummy. Mum was not impressed and kept telling me to get my nose out of the bag.

I listened to Mum and Dad talking in the evening. I'm going to have my first birthday next week. I remember Rosie's birthday and she got a balloon and we all got a really nice tea. I hope I get something nice for my birthday. I do know that I was born the day before Mum's old boy went to rainbow bridge so I have decided I will be really silly next week to try and take her mind off it and to try and stop her from feeling sad. I know I will find a way.

In the evening, we all cuddled up on the sofa and watched Luke finish off the plastering, it was a late night by the time he went home. I was very glad to get to bed tonight. I fell asleep thinking about what my special birthday tea would be.

Tuesday 30th April

I woke up this morning and had the usual routine, breakfast and play with Mum. We were all quite tired because of our late night of plastering but I managed to still get my morning Mum cuddles so all was ok.

Mum went off to work and Dad started to tidy up the bathroom and kitchen, it look him a long time and he took everything out to the car, he filled the boot of the car and I was most upset. That's where I ride when we go out so I guessed we weren't going to the field today, that was ok as long as we went out I didn't care how we got there.

Mum came home early today and helped with the clearing up. She looks a bit sad at the moment and I hear her talking about Zak a fair bit. I really hope she isn't sad on my birthday and after all I was also a pup in need and even though I know they loved Zak so much, he is now having fun at rainbow bridge and isn't hurting anymore. I gave mum extra cuddles today. I know she will be ok.

In the evening she planted more stuff and I was really good and didn't interfere. We had tea and then all cuddled up on the sofa for the rest of the evening. We were all very tired and were glad to get to bed.

Wednesday 1st May

I got up this morning and went out for a wee. I came back in and found one of my favourite cat toys, a little plastic ball with a bell in it. I played for a while and Mum took it off me saying 6Am was too early for play time. I knew it was in her dressing gown pocket so I stamped on her lap for a while to try and get it back. I couldn't. I even tried to chew through the pocket, but then Mum went into the bathroom and got ready for work. Darn it. I lost the ball.

After Mum went to work I watched Dad do cementing on the floor, I really wanted to do a paw print in it but wasn't allowed. I think they should have let me as I noticed there were cement Christmas paw prints on the tree at Christmas time and there wasn't one of mine.

Mum came home and started to cover the walls in white stuff. It was very interesting. I had a taste but it wasn't very nice. I watched her paint for ages. It was fascinating. After she finished she washed all the things she had been using. I went to get a better look and stole a pad thing. I am proud to say I chewed it up! Mum was not impressed. Mum told Dad I was naughty. It was all starting to get very messy and untidy so I decided that I would have a very early night. So I went off to bed.

Thursday 2nd May

I got up this morning and went out for a wee as per usual. Well, I have now learnt to wee like a big boy and I am very good at standing on three legs. I can't believe I didn't work this out sooner. I can also aim my wee to go where ever I want. I came in and had a cuddle with Mum while she had her morning coffee and even played with her for a bit. She said I am like a baby in a big body. I really do like being this big. It's great.

Mum went to work and Dad carried on wrecking the house. I decided to go and sit outside and enjoy the sunshine and left Dad to it. Rosie came and joined me and I lay in the sun with her thinking how lucky I am to have her. I have been doing a lot of thinking about how life was when I was a puppy and all the things I have now learnt. I also know I have a lot more to learn yet.

In the evening we all cuddled up on the sofa and watched tv until it was time to go to bed.

Friday 3rd May

I got up this morning and went out for my usual wee. I came back in for my cuddles and played with her until she went off to work. Dad carried on wrecking the house again today and got really quite angry with the wood bits at the bottom of the walls.

I heard him talking to Mum on the phone and he said he couldn't do it. Mum told him to go and sit down and she would arrange something.

Mum came back early and had lots of flowers with her. She also said she had spoken to Jamie and he was coming over to help Dad with the wood tonight. I was really excited as I like it when Jamie comes over. While I waited for Jamie, I watched Mum arrange all the flowers into a thing to hold in your hand. She started to cut flowers off our hedge as well. I didn't like that so I told Mum to stop. She didn't.

Later on Jamie arrived with tools and stuff, I was so excited to I went and helped him. I carried away the little bits of wood and followed Jamie around so I could check he was doing everything properly. At one point Jamie got cross with me as while he was bent over his bum was showing. I had a sniff and then decided to lick it to see what it tasted like. Jamie told me off and Mum and Dad laughed a lot.

They worked hard all evening and when Jamie finally went home we all went to bed. I was glad to get in my crate away from all the mess.

Saturday 4th May

I got up this morning and had a very quick cuddle with Mum, she was ruching about like a mad woman and playing with the flowers again. She ended up putting them all in a box and then she went out. When she came home she had flowers in her hair.

A while later while Mum was upstairs, Aunty Bean also turned up with flowers in her hair, I thought she looked very pretty, Mum came downstairs and was wearing a yellow dress and had all the flowers she had played with. Aunty Bean looked really happy and said they were lovely and then they went out.

The next thing was Dad, he went upstairs and then came down looking like I have never seen him before. Everything he was wearing matched. Rosie told me it was called a suit and that Dad would probably be going out too. She was right. Dad went out and we all settled down for a sleep.

Mum and Dad were gone for ages. Dad came home first and gave us our tea and we had a long cuddle. I think it is the longest we have ever been home alone, but I was a good boy and Dad told me so. We cuddled up on the sofa with him and all waited for Mum to come home. By the time she got home I was very tired so I said hello and then went off to bed. I was very tired.

Sunday 5th May

Well, this morning was weird. There was no Hollyoaks as Dad had broken the tv a few days before. Jamie came over on his motorbike and then him and Dad went out. Mum started to pain again, so I helped her, but I ended up with paint all over me and especially on my ear and beard.

Mum put the blankets out for us as it was sunny so we all decided to go out and leave her to it. She painted the whole room pretty much by the time Dad and Jamie got back.

Jamie then started to play with the wood again, they were putting new bits down and using big tools to screw them in place. I tried to help but I wasn't allowed. I just ended up following him around again but it was really interesting to see what he was doing. When Jamie went to the loo for a wee, I broke in and watched him. Mum explained to Jamie that they have a lock on the door now to stop me gate crashing people when they go to the toilet. I think they were very mean doing that.

Mum bought fish and chips for everyone rather than cook. I was so gutted to miss my roast but the fish and chips tasted wonderful. I really liked that.

Dad and Jamie worked hard into the evening so I decided to just hang out with Mum on the sofa. I stayed there until bed time as I was so tired from trying to help Jamie all day.

Monday 6th May

I got up this morning and was confused. Mum was at home again today and after her coffee she started to paint again. Dad joined in and helped. I stayed on the sofa for a while with Rosie so Mum had to work around us. We would never give up the sofa for anything. It was a pretty boring day for us really, we did manage to go out but after that we just watched the diy thing for the rest of the day.

I didn't really have that much to report for today, although we did get a lovely roast dinner. I was a bit confused though as that should have been yesterday. Everything just seems a bit out of sorts at the moment. I hope things get back to normal soon.

In the evening I cuddled up with Mum on the sofa, but we didn't watch tv as Dad broke it earlier. I was glad to get back into my crate tonight as that was about the only thing in the house that was still normal.

Tuesday 7th May

I got up this morning and had a quick wee, I then went and had a cuddle with Mum on the sofa before she went to work. I heard her tell Dad that she would be home earlier today. Yippee, I was happy to hear that. Dad did a bit of tidying until Mum came home.

Mum came home and looked a bit cheesed off, every now and then something on her arm started to make strange noises, she told me it was

204

a blood pressure monitor. It was going off every half hour and it made Mum's arm hurt as I kept hearing her say ouch.

After a while there was a knock at the door. It was Parsla, I was very happy to see her. We all ran up to her and gave her cuddles. Although I would come to regret that soon enough.

Mum and Parsla started to look at the sofa, they started to take it to bits, then to our utter disgust, they started to take it out of the house bit by bit until the floor was bare. Me and Rosie just stood there looking and wondering why they had taken our sofa away.

Then it got even worse to be fair. Mum bought in these two plastic things and started to blow them up, they looked like little beds. Apparently the correct name is lilo. They blew them up and rested them against the wall, I could tell that they did that to stop us getting on them. We were just so shocked to have no sofa.

After Parsla went I decided to have a proper sniff of these lilos, then I got disgusted again, I could smell Dad on one of them, but worse than that I could smell another dog. There was only one thing I could do. I lifted my back leg up and peed over it. How dare I smell another dog with Dad's smell?

Dad then told me off but I could see Mum laughing at me. She thought it was funny. She went and got a cloth and cleaned the lilo and the floor.

In the evening Mum did tea and they sat at the table to eat. After that they put up the new tv, it's much bigger than the old one. Mum and Dad lay on the lilos to watch tv and me and Rosie showed them that we were still really annoyed that our sofa was gone. Everybody knows that lurchers need sofas.

I went to bed tonight a bit fed up with the mess and lack of sofa. I was just totally clueless about what was going on and so I thought sleep was the best option.

Wednesday 8th May

Mum came downstairs this morning and greeted me in a completely different way. Mum said Happy Birthday to me. Today I am a whole year old! Mum gave me a hug and a kiss and a chew. She was in a lot of pain with the thing on her arm so she took it off and put it in a packet. When Dad got up he was really nice to me and also said happy birthday. Well. If it's my birthday and you get presents, I would very much like a new sofa.

Mum went off to work and Dad started to clear the house and tidy up. A while later a man came in and put a new carpet down in the front room. It was very lovely and soft so II decided I would stay in the front room and get used to the new carpet. Another man also turned up and put new lights in, this house doesn't look the same anymore. I wasn't sure if I liked it as I loved my sofa and now we have to sit on the floor.

Mum came home and gave me some treats and a bottle of doggy wine and said it was from Claire at work. Mum poured my drink into a wineglass and then I drank it. It got even better at tea time. Dad cooked a massive beef steak, it smelled wonderful and then to my surprise he cut it up and put it in our bowls. We had steak for tea. Rosie explained to me that we get special things on our birthdays. Now, I can't say that I disagree with that.

I learned that a birthday is celebrating the day you were born. I don't remember that much about it but I do know that I was born in a rescue centre and that my puppyhood was at the rescue centre until I was fostered. We had to leave our mum early as she was too weak from having me and my brothers and sisters and needed to get strong again. We were then looked after by a lovely man and lady who looked after us until the day Mum and Dad came to get me. I had to watch all my brothers and sisters leave with their new Mums and Dad's and at one point I though no one would ever want me.

I'm so glad they came to get me though and my new family have taught me so much. The only one thing about today that I felt let the day down was that I had no sofa to lay on.

I went to bed tonight feeling loved, happy and spoilt with good food, so only one birthday wish didn't come true. I didn't get a sofa!

Epilogue

Well, I hope you have enjoyed reading my tales. Today is the 9th of May and I just had to get this in. I got my new sofa today!!!!! I am such a happy boy, it is even bigger than the last one so now I can really stretch out and get comfortable.

The last year for me as been full of great times but also a bit of sadness, I was really sad to leave my real Mum but understand that as a puppy I needed to find my own family and find my own feet too. I have learnt so much in this short time, I know that people are great and generally loving, but I also know there are some people that are not so nice which then leads to families like mine to have to be rescued. I also know it takes a lot of money to keep rescuing dogs like me which is why I decided to write down my story and hope that people will like it and then the money will go to where I was born to help other dogs find forever homes like I got.

Thank you for reading my story, and you never know, I may be back again at some point with more tales to tell, but for now I shall be spending the summer with all my new family and know I am very safe and loved, and I shall really enjoy cuddling up on my new epic sofa.

Harley D Harris.

Printed in Great Britain
by Amazon